THE DAILY HE

THE DAILY

HENRY DAVID
THOREAU

A YEAR OF

QUOTES

FROM THE MAN WHO
LIVED IN SEASON

Edited and with a Foreword by
LAURA DASSOW WALLS

The University of Chicago Press ✳ *Chicago and London*

The University of Chicago Press, Chicago 60637
The University of Chicago Press, Ltd., London
© 2020 by The University of Chicago
Published 2020
Printed in the United States of America

29 28 27 26 25 24 23 22 21 20 1 2 3 4 5

ISBN-13: 978-0-226-62496-9 (paper)
ISBN-13: 978-0-226-62501-0 (e-book)
DOI: https://doi.org/10.7208/chicago/9780226625010.001.0001

Library of Congress Cataloging-in-Publication Data
Names: Thoreau, Henry David, 1817–1862, author. | Walls,
 Laura Dassow, editor.
Title: The daily Henry David Thoreau : a year of quotes from
 the man who lived in season / Henry David Thoreau, Laura
 Dassow Walls.
Description: Chicago : University of Chicago Press, 2020. |
 Includes index.
Identifiers: LCCN 2019024359 | ISBN 9780226624969 (paperback)
 | ISBN 9780226625010 (ebook)
Subjects: LCSH: Thoreau, Henry David, 1817–1862—
 Quotations.
Classification: LCC PS3042 .W27 2020 | DDC 818/.309—dc23
LC record available at https://lccn.loc.gov/2019024359

♾ This paper meets the requirements of ANSI/NISO Z39.48-
1992 (Permanence of Paper).

Foreword

Living in Season

Modernity rules our lives by clock and calendar, dividing the stream of time into ever-smaller units and coordinating our social lives with those around the globe. Henry David Thoreau resisted modernity by using clock and calendar not to segment and regulate time's passing but to open and explore time's presence. Instead of the dead face of the clock, he turned to the living sundial of the world, which tells not artificial time but the active arrival of each moment of each season. His friend Ralph Waldo Emerson noted with awe that from the flowers alone, Thoreau could tell the calendar date within two days; children remembered long into adulthood how Thoreau showed them white water lilies awakening not by clock time but at the first touch of the sun, suggesting how a single moment could index eternity. As Thoreau wrote in *Walden*, "Time is but the stream I go a-fishing in. I drink at it; but while I drink I see the sandy bottom and detect how shallow it is" (see the entry for July).

The Daily Henry David Thoreau explores Thoreau's experiments with the passage and presence of time—in particular, with the lifelong pun he elab-

orated in *Wild Fruits*, his unfinished final work on the cycle of the seasons (see also the entry for August 23):

> Live in each season as it passes; breathe the air, drink the drink, taste the fruit, and resign your-self to the influences of each. . . . Be blown on by all the winds. Open all your pores and bathe in all the tides of Nature, in all her streams and oceans, at all seasons. . . . Grow green with spring, yellow and ripe with autumn. . . . Some men think that they are not well in spring or summer or autumn or winter; (if you will excuse the pun) it is only because they are not indeed *well*; that is, fairly *in* those seasons.

Thoreau's notion of "living in season" sets the key-note for this collection. These quotes invite us to pay full attention to each moment as it passes, with all our senses, taste and touch and smell as well as sight and hearing—to attend to the phenomenology of the great cycles of growth, decay, and renewal. This slender volume thus embodies, in small com-pass, Thoreau's own ambition to write "a book of the seasons, each page of which should be written in its own season and out-of-doors, or in its own locality wherever it may be" (see the entry for June 11). Such a book could have been, in other hands, the dullest of records. Thoreau himself grew up with the familiar "it's winter, so it's snowing" cycle-of-the-seasons repetition, already a cliché of nature writ-ing. He sought far more than this: by keeping a daily

journal of the physical world, he hoped to open the gift of each day, discovering, in the repetitions of mundane cycles, endless variation and surprise. To him, one moment of true observation could catch the cosmos in its flight.

This means that living in season is metaphysical as well, what Thoreau called a "meteorological journal of the mind" (August 18, 1851, *Journal* 2:403). Thoreau's published journal, the source for most of the quotations included here, is just such a work of the observing imagination: its meditations explore what the modern American poet Robert Frost, in his poem "Tree at My Window," referred to as inner and outer weather.

Sometimes the outer dominates, conveyed with just a kick of metaphysical speculation; other times inner weather takes over, often registering the climate of political thought swirling around Thoreau in these darkening years, when abolitionist politics were drawing him and his countrymen into the tragedy of civil war.

But Thoreau saw such political division as a symptom of a still larger war, one already going on all around him: the war between Man and Nature. Even then, New England was deep in the throes of the industrial capitalist revolution, and Thoreau's hometown of Concord, Massachusetts, was right on the front lines. His writings record the environmental devastation wrought by deforestation: his Walden house looked out on clear-cuts, and by the time *Walden* was published, nearly all the woods he'd

known as a child were gone. He documented the pollution dumped by upriver lumber mills and the damage done to fish populations by the industrial dams downriver, as well as the floods which drowned the river meadows on which farmers relied for wild-grown hay. Once he accidentally set fire to the woods, and for the rest of his life he watched closely as the trees regenerated—and as new fires were sparked by the wheels of the railroad trains, burning yet more of the woods. From both his Walden house and his family's home in town, he observed railroad cars carrying New England's resources down to the docks of Boston, returning with products imported from around the world. Globalization was already over-turning his landscape, rearranging the lives of all its inhabitants.

Living in season became Thoreau's way of fight-ing back. He dedicated himself to paying the closest attention to the most minute particulars of nature, at first in order to understand the resiliency of nature's regenerative processes, but then to show his friends what he'd learned. Thoreau taught them how living in season could heal the modern sense of disconti-nuity with one's surroundings, replacing alienation with engagement, negligence with love, ignorance with stewardship. He identified with the sense of wonder he saw in local children, and he vowed he would never grow up and lose his own sense of a world enchanted. This became, as he matured, a profound, even a religious commitment. Thoreau devoted himself to attuning body and mind toward

reaching a mystical oneness with the natural world, even as his painstaking researches took on the character of science. (His essay "The Succession of Forest Trees" remains a foundational text of forest ecology.)

Through all this, writing was always at the core: Thoreau vowed to be "the scribe of all nature . . . the corn and the grass and the atmosphere writing" (see the entry for September 2). His thoughts live on because of his passion for the wild, but also because of his love for language, which he tuned with a scholar's precision and a musician's ear. Thanks to his writing, his world lives on, a gift that teaches how we, too, can relate the local specifics of our environment with the larger climate of our times and discover, even in a fallen world, a beauty worth defending.

A Very Brief Thoreau Chronology

1817	July 12: born in Concord, MA
1823	Thoreau family moves back to Concord after living elsewhere in Massachusetts; father John Thoreau Sr. starts pencil manufacturing business
1828–33	Attends Concord Academy
1833–37	Attends Harvard College
1837	October 22: begins keeping his journal
1838–41	Runs the Concord Academy with his brother John
1841–43	Lives in the Concord home of Ralph Waldo Emerson
1842	January 11: Thoreau's brother John dies of tetanus, age 26
1843	May–December: lives on Staten Island, NY, while tutoring for William Emerson
1844	April 30: accidentally sets fire to Walden Woods, burning about 150 acres
1845	July 4: moves to Walden Pond, living in a house he built himself
1846	July 23: jailed for one night for nonpayment of taxes
1847	September 6: leaves Walden to live with the Emerson family while Ralph Waldo Emerson lectures abroad
1848	July 30: moves back in with his family

THE DAILY HENRY DAVID THOREAU

JANUARY

After a still winter night I awoke with the impression
that some question had been put to me, which I had
been endeavoring in vain to answer in my sleep, as
what—how—when—where? But there was dawning
Nature, in whom all creatures live, looking in at my
broad windows with serene and satisfied face, and
no question on *her* lips. I awoke to an answered ques-
tion, to Nature and daylight. The snow lying deep on
the earth dotted with young pines, and the very slope
of the hill on which my house is placed, seemed to
say, Forward! Nature puts no question and answers
none which we mortals ask.

"The Pond in Winter," *Walden* (1854)

JANUARY 1

Mercury down to 13° below zero.... The winter, cold and bound out as it is, is thrown to us like a bone to a famishing dog, and we are expected to get the marrow out of it.... But the winter was not given to us for no purpose. We must thaw its cold with our genialness.... It is for man the seasons and all their fruits exist. The winter was made to concentrate and harden and mature the kernel of his brain, to give tone and firmness and consistency to his thought. Then is the great harvest of the year, the harvest of thought.

JANUARY 2

The bells are particularly sweet this morning. I hear more, methinks, than ever before. How much more religion in their sound, than they ever call men together to! Men obey their call and go to the stove-warmed church, though God exhibits himself to the walker in a frosted bush to-day, as much as in a burning one to Moses of old.

JANUARY 3

I love Nature partly *because* she is not man, but a retreat from him. None of his institutions control or pervade her. There a different kind of right prevails. In her midst I can be glad with an entire gladness. If this world were all man, I could not stretch myself, I should lose all hope. He is constraint, she is freedom to me. He makes me wish for another world. She makes me content with this.... The joy which Nature yields is like [that] afforded by the frank words of one we love.

JANUARY 4

The fates are wild, for they *will*; and the Almighty is wild above all, as fate is.

JANUARY 5

Very little evidence of God or man did I see just then, and life not as rich and inviting an enterprise as it should be, when my attention was caught by a snow-flake on my coat-sleeve. It was one of those perfect, crystalline, star-shaped ones, six-rayed, like a flat

wheel with six spokes, only the spokes were perfect little pine trees in shape, arranged around a central spangle..... These little wheels came down like the wrecks of chariots from a battle waged in the sky.... We are rained and snowed on with gems.

JANUARY 6
JOURNAL (JANUARY 5, 1856)

The same law that shapes the earth-star shapes the snow-star. As surely as the petals of a flower are fixed, each of these countless snow-stars comes whirling to earth, pronouncing thus, with emphasis, the number six. Order, Κόσμος [Cosmos]. . . . Meanwhile the meadow mouse shoves them aside in his gallery, the schoolboy casts them in his snowball, or the woodman's sled glides smoothly over them, these glorious spangles, the sweeping of heaven's floor. And they all sing, melting as they sing of the mysteries of the number six,—six, six, six.

JANUARY 7
JOURNAL* (AFTER JANUARY 5, 1850)

I have no satisfaction in the visits of some of my acquaintances because they do not make themselves at home—Sit down & sit heavy though you

break my chairs. If you have leisure to be met I will meet you. I will not take you on the wing. If you have any engagement—fulfill it & leave me. Unless you abound in leisure as the creator when he made this globe—Farewell.

JANUARY 8
JOURNAL (JANUARY 8, 1860)

We are suddenly surrounded by a warm air from some other part of the globe. What a change! . . . You cannot listen a moment such a day as this but you will hear, from far or near, the clarion of the cock celebrating this new season, yielding to the influence of the south wind, or the drawling note of the hen dreaming of eggs that are to be. . . . They are affected like voyagers on approaching the land. We discover a new world every time that we see the earth again after it has been covered for a season with snow.

JANUARY 9
"FORMER INHABITANTS; AND
WINTER VISITORS," *WALDEN* (1854)

The one who came from farthest to my lodge, through deepest snows and most dismal tempests, was a poet. A farmer, a hunter, a soldier, a reporter,

even a philosopher, may be daunted; but nothing can deter a poet, for he is actuated by pure love.

JANUARY 10

A cold and searching wind drives away all contagion, and nothing can withstand it but what has a virtue in it, and accordingly, whatever we meet with in cold and bleak places, as the tops of mountains, we respect for a sort of sturdy innocence, a Puritan toughness. All things beside seem to be called in for shelter, and what stays out must be part of the original frame of the universe, and of such valor as God himself.

JANUARY 11

JOURNAL (JANUARY 12, 1854)

Every winter the surface of the pond to the depth of a foot becomes solid so as to support the heaviest teams, and anon the snow covers it to an equal depth, so that it is not to be distinguished from a level field. Thus, like the marmots in the surrounding hills, it too closes its eyelids and becomes partially dormant.

JANUARY 12
JOURNAL (JANUARY 12, 1855)

Perhaps what most moves us in winter is some reminiscence of far-off summer. How we leap by the side of the open brooks! What beauty in the running brooks! What life! What society! The cold is merely superficial; it is summer still at the core, far, far within. It is in the cawing of the crow, the crowing of the cock, the warmth of the sun on our backs. . . . What a delicious sound! It is not merely crow calling to crow, for it speaks to me too. I am part of one great creature with him; if he has voice, I have ears.

JANUARY 13
JOURNAL (JANUARY 1851)

I am struck by the fact that no work has been shirked when a piece of cloth is produced, every thread has been counted in the finest web. . . . The arts teach us a thousand lessons. Not a yard of cloth can be woven without the most thorough fidelity in the weaver. The ship must be made *absolutely* tight before it is launched.

JANUARY 14

I can see at a distance above the level of the snow a few bushes and grasses which mark the edge of the river. They seem to write the word *rivus* there.

JANUARY 15

"ECONOMY," *WALDEN* (1854)

In any weather, at any hour of the day or night, I have been anxious to improve the nick of time, and notch it on my stick too; to stand on the meeting of two eternities, the past and future, which is precisely the present moment; to toe that line.

JANUARY 16

JOURNAL (JANUARY 1, 1854)

We might expect to find in the snow the footprint of a life superior to our own, of which no zoölogy takes cognizance.... A life which has not gone by and left a footprint merely, but all that we see is the impress of its spirit, is there with its beauty, its music, its perfume, its sweetness, to exhilarate and recreate us.... Is there no trace of intelligence there? ... No other trail but such as a dog can smell?

JANUARY 17
JOURNAL (JANUARY 17, 1860)

Alcott said well the other day that this was his definition of heaven, "A place where you can have a little conversation."

JANUARY 18
JOURNAL (JANUARY 18, 1856)

This is a very mild, melting winter day, but clear and bright, yet I see the blue shadows on the snow at Walden. The snow lies very level there, about ten inches deep, and for the most part bears me as I go across with my hatchet. I think I never saw a more elysian blue than my shadow. I am turned into a tall blue Persian from my cap to my boots, such as no mortal dye can produce, with an amethystine hatchet in my hand. I am in raptures at my own shadow.

JANUARY 19
"HOUSE-WARMING," *WALDEN* (1854)

Every man looks at his wood-pile with a kind of affection. I loved to have mine before my window, and the more chips the better to remind me of my pleasing work.

JANUARY 20

JOURNAL (JANUARY 20, 1852)

The farmers nowadays can cart out peat and muck over the frozen meadows. Somewhat analogous, methinks, the scholar does; drives in with tight-braced energy and winter cheer on to his now firm meadowy grounds, and carts, hauls off, the virgin loads of fertilizing soil which he threw up in the warm, soft summer. . . . The scholar's and the farmer's work are strictly analogous. . . . He is doing like myself. My barn-yard is my journal.

JANUARY 21

JOURNAL (JANUARY 21, 1853)

The blueness of the sky at night—the color it wears by day—is an everlasting surprise to me, suggesting the constant presence and prevalence of light in the firmament, that we see through the veil of night to the constant blue, as by day. The night is not black when the air is clear, but blue still. The great ocean of light and ether is unaffected by our partial night. Night is not universal. At midnight I see into the universal day.

JANUARY 22

JOURNAL (JANUARY 21, 1853)

As I walk the railroad causeway I am, as the last two months, disturbed by the sound of my steps on the frozen ground. I wish to hear the silence of the night, for the silence is something positive and to be heard. I cannot walk with my ears covered. . . . As I leave the village, drawing nearer to the woods, I listen from time to time to hear the hounds of Silence baying the Moon,—to know if they are on the track of any game. . . . The silence rings; it is musical and thrills me. A night in which the silence was audible. I hear the unspeakable.

JANUARY 23

JOURNAL (JANUARY 23, 1841)

A day is lapsing. I hear cockerels crowing in the yard, and see them stalking among the chips in the sun. I hear busy feet on the floors, and the whole house jars with industry. Surely the day is well spent, and the time is full to overflowing.

JANUARY 24

JOURNAL (JANUARY 24, 1858)

The river is broadly open, as usual this winter. You

can hardly say that we have had any sleighing at all this winter. . . . I do not quite like this warm weather and bare ground at this season. What is a winter without snow and ice in this latitude? The bare earth is unsightly. This winter is but unburied summer.

JANUARY 25
JOURNAL (JANUARY 21, 1852)

This winter they are cutting down our woods more seriously than ever,—Fair Haven Hill, Walden, Linnaea Borealis Wood, etc., etc. Thank God, they cannot cut down the clouds!

JANUARY 26
JOURNAL (JANUARY 27, 1854)

You tell me that you are growing old and are troubled to see without glasses, but this is unimportant if the divine faculty of the seer shows no signs of decay.

JANUARY 27
JOURNAL (JANUARY 27, 1852)

I do not know but thoughts written down thus in

a journal might be printed in the same form with greater advantage than if the related ones were brought together into separate essays. They are now allied to life, and are seen by the reader not to be far-fetched. It is more simple, less artful. . . . Mere facts and names and dates communicate more than we suspect. Whether the flower looks better in the nosegay than in the meadow where it grew and we had to wet our feet to get it!

JANUARY 28
JOURNAL (JANUARY 27, 1860)

When you think that your walk is profitless and a failure, and you can hardly persuade yourself not to return, it is on the point of being a success, for then you are in that subdued and knocking mood to which Nature never fails to open.

JANUARY 29
JOURNAL (JANUARY 30, 1860)

The crow, flying high, touches the tympanum of the sky for us, and reveals the tone of it.

JANUARY 30

I knew a crazy man who walked into an empty pulpit one Sunday and, taking up a hymn-book, remarked: "We have had a good fall for getting in corn and potatoes. Let us sing Winter." So I say, "Let us sing winter." What else can we sing, and our voices be in harmony with the season?

JANUARY 31

We too have our thaws. They come to our January moods, when our ice cracks, and our sluices break loose. Thought that was frozen up under stern experience gushes forth in feeling and expression. This is a freshet which carries away dams of accumulated ice. Our thoughts hide unexpressed, like the buds under their downy or resinous scales; they would hardly keep a partridge from starving. If you would know what are my winter thoughts look for them in the partridge's crop.

FEBRUARY

The earth is not a mere fragment of dead history, stratum upon stratum like the leaves of a book, to be studied by geologists and antiquaries chiefly, but living poetry like the leaves of a tree, which precede flowers and fruit,—not a fossil earth, but a living earth; compared with whose great central life all animal and vegetable life is merely parasitic. Its throes will heave our exuviae from their graves. You may melt your metals and cast them into the most beautiful moulds you can; they will never excite me like the forms which this molten earth flows out into. And not only it, but the institutions upon it are plastic like clay in the hands of the potter.

"Spring," *Walden* (1854)

FEBRUARY 1

"WALKING" (1862)

Above all, we cannot afford not to live in the present. He is blessed over all mortals who loses no moment of the passing life in remembering the past. Unless our philosophy hears the cock crow in every barnyard within our horizon, it is belated. That sound commonly reminds us that we are growing rusty and antique in our employments and habits of thought. His philosophy comes down to a more recent time than ours. There is something suggested by it that is a newer testament,—the gospel according to this moment.

FEBRUARY 2

"THE POND IN WINTER," *WALDEN* (1854)

In the morning I bathe my intellect in the stupendous and cosmogonal philosophy of the Bhagvat-Geeta, since whose composition years of the gods have elapsed, and in comparison with which our modern world and its literature seem puny and trivial. . . . I lay down the book and go to my well for water, and lo! there I meet the servant of the Bramin, priest of Brahma and Vishnu and Indra, who still sits in his temple on the Ganges reading the Vedas, or dwells at the root of a tree with his crust and water jug. . . . Our buckets as it were grate together in the

same well. The pure Walden water is mingled with the sacred water of the Ganges.

FEBRUARY 3
JOURNAL (FEBRUARY 3, 1855)

Some little boys ten years old are as handsome skaters as I know. They sweep along with a graceful floating motion, leaning now to this side, then to that, like a marsh hawk beating the bush.

FEBRUARY 4
JOURNAL (FEBRUARY 5, 1855)

In a journal it is important in a few words to describe the weather, or character of the day, as it affects our feelings. That which was so important at the time cannot be unimportant to remember.

FEBRUARY 5
"WALKING" (1862)

Where is the literature which gives expression to Nature? He would be a poet who could impress the winds and streams into his service, to speak for him;

. . . whose words were so true and fresh and natural that they would appear to expand like the buds at the approach of spring.

FEBRUARY 6

"ECONOMY," *WALDEN* (1854)

When we consider what, to use the words of the catechism, is the chief end of man, and what are the true necessaries and means of life, it appears as if men had deliberately chosen the common mode of living because they preferred it to any other. Yet they honestly think there is no choice left. But alert and healthy natures remember that the sun rose clear. It is never too late to give up our prejudices.

FEBRUARY 7

JOURNAL (FEBRUARY 7, 1855)

The coldest night for a long, long time was last. Sheets froze stiff about the faces. Cat mewed to have the door opened, but was at first disinclined to go out. When she came in at nine she smelt of meadow-hay. We all took her up and smelled of her, it was so fragrant. Had cuddled in some barn. People dreaded to go to bed. The ground cracked in the night as if a powder-mill had blown up, and the timbers of the

house also. My pail of water was frozen in the morning so that I could not break it. Must leave many buttons unbuttoned, owing to numb fingers. [THOREAU WAS THEN LIVING WITH HIS FAMILY IN CONCORD.]

FEBRUARY 8
JOURNAL (FEBRUARY 8, 1841)

Every man proposes fairly, and does not willfully take the devil for his guide; as our shadows never fall between us and the sun. Go towards the sun and your shadow will fall behind you.

FEBRUARY 9
JOURNAL (FEBRUARY 9, 1852)

The state of the atmosphere is continually varying, and, to a keen observer, objects do not twice present exactly the same appearance. If I invert my head this morning and look at the woods in the horizon, they do not look so far off and elysian-like as in the afternoon. . . . The prospect is thus actually a constantly varying mirage, answering to the condition of our perceptive faculties and our fluctuating imaginations. . . . A man goes to the end of his garden, inverts his head, and does not know his own cottage. The novelty is in us, and it is also in nature.

FEBRUARY 10

"ECONOMY," *WALDEN* (1854)

A lady once offered me a mat, but as I had no room to spare within the house, nor time to spare within or without to shake it, I declined it, preferring to wipe my feet on the sod before my door. It is best to avoid the beginnings of evil.

FEBRUARY 11

JOURNAL (FEBRUARY 11, 1852)

Perhaps the best evidence of an amelioration of the climate—at least that the snows are less deep than formerly—is the snow-shoes which still lie about in so many garrets, now useless, though the population of this town has not essentially increased for seventy-five years past, and the travelling within the limits of the town accordingly not much facilitated. No man ever uses them now, yet the old men used them in their youth.

FEBRUARY 12

"SPRING," *WALDEN* (1854)

The pond began to boom about an hour after sunrise, when it felt the influence of the sun's rays

slanted upon it from over the hills; it stretched itself and yawned like a waking man with a gradually increasing tumult, which was kept up three or four hours. . . . The pond does not thunder every evening, and I cannot tell surely when to expect its thundering; but though I may perceive no difference in the weather, it does. Who would have suspected so large and cold and thick-skinned a thing to be so sensitive? Yet it has its law to which it thunders obedience when it should as surely as the buds expand in the spring. The earth is all alive and covered with papillae. The largest pond is as sensitive to atmospheric changes as the globule of mercury in its tube.

[ORIGINALLY WRITTEN ON FEBRUARY 12, 1854.]

FEBRUARY 13
"ECONOMY," *WALDEN* (1854)

To meet the objections of some inveterate cavillers, I may as well state, that if I dined out occasionally, as I always had done, and I trust shall have opportunities to do again, it was frequently to the detriment of my domestic arrangements.

FEBRUARY 14

JOURNAL (JULY 25, 1839)

There is no remedy for love but to love more.

FEBRUARY 15

"A YANKEE IN CANADA" (1866)

I shall never again wake up in a colder night than usual, but I shall think how rapidly the sentinels are relieving one another on the walls of Quebec, their quicksilver being all frozen, as if apprehensive that some hostile Wolfe may even then be scaling the Heights of Abraham, or some persevering Arnold about to issue from the wilderness; some Malay or Japanese, perchance, coming round by the north-west coast, have chosen that moment to assault the citadel! . . . What a troublesome thing a wall is! I thought it was to defend me, and not I it!

FEBRUARY 16

JOURNAL (FEBRUARY 8, 1841)

All we have experienced is so much gone within us, and there lies. It is the company we keep. One day, in health or sickness, it will come out and be remembered. Neither body nor soul forgets anything. The

twig always remembers the wind that shook it, and the stone the cuff it received. Ask the old tree and the sand.

FEBRUARY 17
JOURNAL (FEBRUARY 19, 1854)

Did not they intend that we should read and ponder, who covered the whole earth with alphabets,— primers or bibles,—coarse or fine print? The very débris of the cliffs—the stivers of the rocks—are covered with geographic lichens: no surface is permitted to be bare long. . . . Print! it is a close-hugging lichen that forms on a favorable surface, which paper offers. The linen gets itself wrought into paper that the song of the shirt may be printed on it. Who placed us with eyes between a microscopic and a telescopic world?

FEBRUARY 18
JOURNAL (FEBRUARY 19, 1855)

If you wish to know how I think, you must endeavor to put yourself in my place. If you wish me to speak as if I were you, that is another affair.

Everywhere snow, gathered into sloping drifts about the walls and fences, and, beneath the snow, the frozen ground, and men are compelled to deposit the summer's provision in burrows in the earth like the ground squirrel. Many creatures, daunted by the prospect, migrated in the fall, but man remains and walks over the frozen snow-crust and over the stiffened rivers and ponds. . . . Life is reduced to its lowest terms. There is no home for you now, in this freezing wind, but in that shelter which you prepared in the summer. You steer straight across the fields to that in season. I can with difficulty tell when I am over the river. There is a similar crust over my heart.

What is the relation between a bird and the ear that appreciates its melody . . . ? Certainly they are intimately related, and the one was made for the other. It is a natural fact. If I were to discover that a certain kind of stone by the pond-shore was affected, say partially disintegrated, by a particular natural sound, as of a bird or insect, I see that one could not be completely described without describing the other. I am that rock by the pond-side.

A warmth begins to be reflected from the partially dried ground here and there in the sun in sheltered places. . . . When I perceive this dryness under my feet, I feel as if I had got a new sense, or rather I realize what was incredible to me before, that there is a new life in Nature beginning to awake, that her halls are being swept and prepared for a new occupant. It is whispered through all the aisles of the forest that another spring is approaching. The wood mouse listens at the mouth of his burrow, and the chickadee passes the news along.

FEBRUARY 22

"ECONOMY," *WALDEN* (1854)

If I seem to boast more than is becoming, my excuse is that I brag for humanity rather than for myself; and my shortcomings and inconsistencies do not affect the truth of my statement. . . . I am resolved that I will not through humility become the devil's attorney. I will endeavor to speak a good word for the truth.

FEBRUARY 23

"WALKING" (1862)

I would not have every man nor every part of a man cultivated, any more than I would have every acre of earth cultivated: part will be tillage, but the greater part will be meadow and forest, not only serving an immediate use, but preparing a mould against a distant future, by the annual decay of the vegetation which it supports.

FEBRUARY 24

"SPRING," *WALDEN* (1854)

A single gentle rain makes the grass many shades greener. So our prospects brighten on the influx of better thoughts.

FEBRUARY 25

A WEEK ON THE CONCORD AND MERRIMACK RIVERS (1849)

Men nowhere, east or west, live yet a *natural* life, round which the vine clings, and which the elm willingly shadows. Man would desecrate it by his touch, and so the beauty of the world remains veiled to him. He needs not only to be spiritualized, but *naturalized*,

on the soil of earth. Who shall conceive what kind of roof the heavens might extend over him, what seasons minister to him, and what employment dignify his life!

FEBRUARY 26

JOURNAL (FEBRUARY 26, 1840)

Corn grows in the night.

FEBRUARY 27

JOURNAL (FEBRUARY 27, 1860)

I must now walk where I can see the most water, as to the most living part of nature. This is the blood of the earth, and we see its blue arteries pulsing with new life now.

FEBRUARY 28

"LIFE WITHOUT PRINCIPLE" (1863)

I do not know but it is too much to read one newspaper a week. I have tried it recently, and for so long it seems to me that I have not dwelt in my native region.

My desire for knowledge is intermittent, but my desire to bathe my head in atmospheres unknown to my feet is perennial and constant. The highest that we can attain to is not Knowledge, but Sympathy with Intelligence. I do not know that this higher knowledge amounts to anything more definite than a novel and grand surprise on a sudden revelation of the insufficiency of all that we called Knowledge before,—a discovery that there are more things in heaven and earth than are dreamed of in our philosophy. It is the lighting up of the mist by the sun.

[ORIGINALLY WRITTEN ON FEBRUARY 27, 1851.]

MARCH

This afternoon I throw off my outside coat. A mild spring day. I must hie to the Great Meadows. The air is full of bluebirds. The ground almost entirely bare. The villagers are out in the sun, and every man is happy whose work takes him outdoors. I go by Sleepy Hollow toward the Great Fields. I lean over a rail to hear what is in the air, liquid with the blue-birds' warble. My life partakes of infinity. . . . I go forth to make new demands on life. I wish to begin this summer well; to do something in it worthy of it and of me. . . . May I dare as I have never done! May I persevere as I have never done! May I purify myself anew as with fire and water, soul and body! May my melody not be wanting to the season!

Journal (March 15, 1852)

MARCH 1
"WALKING" (1862)

How little appreciation of the beauty of the land-
scape there is among us! We have to be told that the
Greeks called the world Κόσμος [Cosmos], Beauty, or
Order, but we do not see clearly why they did so, and
we esteem it at best only a curious philological fact.

MARCH 2
JOURNAL (MARCH 2, 1859)

The bluebird which some woodchopper or inspired
walker is said to have seen in that sunny interval
between the snow-storms is like a speck of clear blue
sky seen near the end of a storm, reminding us of an
ethereal region and a heaven which we had forgot-
ten. . . . His soft warble melts in the ear, as the snow
is melting in the valleys around. The bluebird comes
and with his warble drills the ice and sets free the riv-
ers and ponds and frozen ground. As the sand flows
down the slopes a little way, assuming the forms of
foliage where the frost comes out of the ground, so
this little rill of melody flows a short way down the
concave of the sky.

MARCH 3

I believe that the mind can be permanently profaned by the habit of attending to trivial things, so that all our thoughts shall be tinged with triviality. Our very intellect shall be macadamized, as it were,—its foundation broken into fragments for the wheels of travel to roll over.

MARCH 4

Entomology extends the limits of being in a new direction, so that I walk in nature with a sense of greater space and freedom. It suggests besides, that the universe is not rough-hewn, but perfect in its details. Nature will bear the closest inspection; she invites us to lay our eye level with the smallest leaf, and take an insect view of its plain. She has no interstices; every part is full of life.

MARCH 5

Channing, talking with Minott the other day about his health, said, "I suppose you'd like to die now." "No," said Minott, "I've toughed it through the win-

ter, and I want to stay and hear the bluebirds once more."

MARCH 6

A WEEK ON THE CONCORD AND MERRIMACK RIVERS (1849)

Much is said about the progress of science in these centuries. I should say that the useful results of science had accumulated, but that there had been no accumulation of knowledge, strictly speaking, for posterity; for knowledge is to be acquired only by a corresponding experience. How can we *know* what we are *told* merely? Each man can interpret another's experience only by his own.

MARCH 7

"WALKING" (1862)

In literature it is only the wild that attracts us. Dullness is but another name for tameness. It is the uncivilized free and wild thinking in Hamlet and the Iliad, in all the scriptures and mythologies, not learned in the schools, that delights us. As the wild duck is more swift and beautiful than the tame, so is the wild—the mallard—thought, which 'mid falling dews wings its way above the fens. A truly good book is something as natural, and as unexpectedly

and unaccountably fair and perfect, as a wild-flower discovered on the prairies of the West or in the jungles of the East.

MARCH 8

JOURNAL (MARCH 10, 1855)

You are always surprised by the sight of the first spring bird or insect; they seem premature, and there is no such evidence of spring as themselves, so that they literally *fetch* the year about. It is thus when I hear the first robin or bluebird or, looking along the brooks, see the first water-bugs out circling. But you think, They have come, and Nature cannot recede.

MARCH 9

JOURNAL (MARCH 9, 1852)

A warm spring rain in the night. . . . Though cloudy, the air excites me. Yesterday all was tight as a stricture on my breast; to-day all is loosened. It is a different element from what it was. The sides of bushy hills where the snow is melted look, through this air, as if I were under the influence of some intoxicating liquor. The earth is not quite steady nor palpable to my sense, a little idealized. . . . The pond is covered with puddles.

MARCH 10

JOURNAL (MARCH 10, 1852)

I see the reticulated leaves of the rattlesnake-plantain in the woods, quite fresh and green. . . . There are some other plants with bright-green leaves which have either started somewhat or have never suffered from the cold under the snow. Summer clenches hands with summer under the snow.

MARCH 11

"SPRING," *WALDEN* (1854)

The first sparrow of spring! The year beginning with younger hope than ever! The faint silvery warblings heard over the partially bare and moist fields from the bluebird, the song sparrow, and the red-wing, as if the last flakes of winter tinkled as they fell! What at such a time are histories, chronologies, traditions, and all written revelations?

MARCH 12

JOURNAL (MARCH 12, 1853)

Some men endeavor to live a constrained life, to subject their whole lives to their wills, as he who said he would give a sign if he were conscious after

his head was cut off,—but he gave no sign. Dwell as near as possible to the channel in which your life flows.

MARCH 13

JOURNAL (MARCH 13, 1859)

I see a small flock of blackbirds flying over, some rising, others falling, yet all advancing together, one flock but many birds, some silent, others tchucking,—incessant alternation. This harmonious movement as in a dance, this agreeing to differ, makes the charm of the spectacle to me. One bird looks fractional, naked, like a single thread or ravelling from the web to which it belongs. Alternation! Alternation! Heaven and hell! Here again in the flight of a bird, its ricochet motion, is that undulation observed in so many materials, as in the mackerel sky.

MARCH 14

"LIFE WITHOUT PRINCIPLE" (1863)

There is no more fatal blunderer than he who consumes the greater part of his life getting his living. All great enterprises are self-supporting. The poet, for instance, must sustain his body by his poetry, as

a steam planing-mill feeds its boilers with the shavings it makes. You must get your living by loving.

[ORIGINALLY WRITTEN ON MARCH 13, 1853.]

MARCH 15

"WHERE I LIVED, AND WHAT I LIVED FOR," *WALDEN* (1854)

God himself culminates in the present moment, and will never be more divine in the lapse of all the ages. And we are enabled to apprehend at all what is sublime and noble only by the perpetual instilling and drenching of the reality that surrounds us. The universe constantly and obediently answers to our conceptions; whether we travel fast or slow, the track is laid for us. Let us spend our lives in conceiving then. The poet or the artist never yet had so fair and noble a design but some of his posterity at least could accomplish it.

MARCH 16

JOURNAL* (AFTER MARCH 11, 1845)

The hunter regards with awe his game and it becomes at last his medicine.

MARCH 17

JOURNAL (MARCH 18, 1858)

Each new year is a surprise to us. We find that we had virtually forgotten the note of each bird, and when we hear it again it is remembered like a dream, reminding us of a previous state of existence.

MARCH 18

JOURNAL (MARCH 18, 1853)

The sun is now declining, with a warm and bright light on all things, a light which answers to the late afterglow of the year, when, in the fall, wrapping his cloak closer about him, the traveller goes home at night to prepare for winter. This the foreglow of the year, when the walker goes home at eve to dream of summer.

To-day first I smelled the earth.

MARCH 19

JOURNAL (MARCH 18, 1853)

I stand still now to listen if I may hear the note of any new bird, for the sound of my steps hinders, and there are so few sounds at this season in a still afternoon like this that you are pretty sure to detect

one within a considerable distance. Hark! Did I not hear the note of some bird then? Methinks it could not have been my own breathing through my nose. No, there it is again,—a robin; and we have put the winter so much further behind us.

MARCH 20
JOURNAL (MARCH 20, 1853)

Walden is melting apace. . . . The wind blows eastward over the opaque ice, unusually hard, . . . all watered or waved like a tessellated floor, a figured carpet; yet dead, yet in vain, till it slides on to the living water surface, where it raises a myriad brilliant sparkles on the bare face of the pond, an expression of glee, of youth, of spring, as if it spoke the joy of the fishes within it and of the sands on its shore, a silvery sheen like the scales of a leuciscus, as if it were all one active fish in the spring. It is the contrast between life and death. There is the difference between winter and spring. [LEUCISCUS IS A COMMON FISH, ALSO CALLED A DACE OR CHUB.]

MARCH 21

JOURNAL (MARCH 21, 1853)

It is a genial and reassuring day; the mere warmth of the west wind amounts almost to balminess. . . . I sit down by a wall to see if I can muse again. We become, as it were, pliant and ductile again to strange but memorable influences; we are led a little way by our genius. We are affected like the earth, and yield to the elemental tenderness; winter breaks up within us; the frost is coming out of me, and I am heaved like the road; accumulated masses of ice and snow dissolve, and thoughts like a freshet pour down unwonted channels. . . . Encouraged, I set out once more to climb the mountain of the earth, for my steps are symbolical steps, and in all my walking I have not reached the top of the earth yet.

MARCH 22

JOURNAL (MARCH 22, 1842)

I have not succeeded if I have an antagonist who fails. It must be humanity's success.

Very significant are the flight of geese and the migration of suckers, etc., etc. But when I consider that the nobler animals have been exterminated here,—the cougar, panther, lynx, wolverene, wolf, bear, moose, deer, the beaver, the turkey, etc., etc.,—I cannot but feel as if I lived in a tamed, and, as it were, emasculated country. . . . When I think what were the various sounds and notes, the migrations and works, and changes of fur and plumage which ushered in the spring and marked the other seasons of the year, I am reminded that this my life in nature, this particular round of natural phenomena which I call a year, is lamentably incomplete. I listen to [a] concert in which so many parts are wanting.

Can you ever be sure that you have heard the very first wood frog in the township croak? Ah! how weather-wise must he be! There is no guessing at the weather with him. . . . The weather, what is it but the temperament of the earth? and he is wholly of the earth, sensitive as its skin in which he lives and of which he is a part. His life relaxes with the thawing ground. He pitches and tunes his voice to chord with the rus-

tling leaves which the March wind has dried. . . . His is the very voice of the weather. He rises and falls like quicksilver in the thermometer.

MARCH 25

JOURNAL (MARCH 25, 1860)

The sleighing, the sledding, or sliding, is gone. We now begin to wheel or roll ourselves and commodities along, which requires more tractile power. The ponderous cart and the spruce buggy appear from out their *latebrae* [lurking places] like the dusty flies that have wintered in a crevice, and we hear the buzzing of their wheels. The high-set chaise, the lumbering coach like wasps and gnats and bees come humming forth.

MARCH 26

"ECONOMY," *WALDEN* (1854)

It is difficult to begin without borrowing, but perhaps it is the most generous course thus to permit your fellow-men to have an interest in your enterprise. The owner of the axe, as he released his hold on it, said that it was the apple of his eye; but I returned it sharper than I received it.

MARCH 27

JOURNAL (MARCH 28, 1859)

Time will soon destroy the works of famous paint-ers and sculptors, but the Indian arrowhead will balk his efforts and Eternity will have come to his aid. They are not fossil bones, but, as it were, fossil thoughts, forever reminding me of the mind that shaped them. . . . The footprint, the mind-print of the oldest men.

MARCH 28

JOURNAL (MARCH 28, 1859)

Our vernal lakes have a beauty to my mind which they would not possess if they were more perma-nent. Everything is in rapid flux here, suggesting that Nature is alive to her extremities and superficies. To-day we sail swiftly on dark rolling waves or paddle over a sea as smooth as a mirror, unable to touch the bottom, where mowers work and hide their jugs in August; coasting the edge of maple swamps, where alder tassels and white maple flowers are kissing the tide that has risen to meet them. But this particu-lar phase of beauty is fleeting. Nature has so many shows for us she cannot afford to give much time to this. In a few days, perchance, these lakes will have all run away to the sea.

MARCH 29

Not till we are completely lost, or turned round,—for a man needs only to be turned round once with his eyes shut in this world to be lost,—do we appreciate the vastness and strangeness of nature. Every man has to learn the points of compass again as often as he awakes, whether from sleep or any abstraction. Not till we are lost, in other words, not till we have lost the world, do we begin to find ourselves, and realize where we are and the infinite extent of our relations. [ORIGINALLY WRITTEN ON MARCH 29, 1853.]

MARCH 30

JOURNAL (MARCH 31, 1858)

Just after sundown I see a large flock of geese in a perfect harrow cleaving their way toward the northeast, with Napoleonic tactics splitting the forces of winter.

MARCH 31

JOURNAL (MARCH 31, 1852)

Methinks I would share every creature's suffering for the sake of its experience and joy. The song sparrow and the transient fox-colored sparrow,—have they

brought me no message this year? . . . God did not make this world in jest; no, nor in indifference. These migrating sparrows all bear messages that concern my life. . . . I love the birds and beasts because they are mythologically in earnest. I see that the sparrow cheeps and flits and sings adequately to the great design of the universe. . . . I reproach myself because I have regarded with indifference the passage of the birds; I have thought them no better than I.

APRIL

The change from storm and winter to serene and mild weather, from dark and sluggish hours to bright and elastic ones, is a memorable crisis which all things proclaim. It is seemingly instantaneous at last. Suddenly an influx of light filled my house, though the evening was at hand, and the clouds of winter still overhung it, and the eaves were dripping with sleety rain. I looked out the window, and lo! where yesterday was cold gray ice there lay the transparent pond already calm and full of hope as on a summer evening, reflecting a summer evening sky in its bosom, though none was visible overhead, as if it had intelligence with some remote horizon.

"Spring," *Walden* (1854)

APRIL 1

On the 1st of April it rained and melted the ice, and in the early part of the day, which was very foggy, I heard a stray goose groping about over the pond and cackling as if lost, or like the spirit of the fog.

APRIL 2

I was sitting on the rail over the brook, when I heard something which reminded me of the song of the robin in rainy days in past springs. Why is it that not the note itself, but something which reminds me of it, should affect me most?—the ideal instead of the actual.

APRIL 3

How novel and original must be each new man's view of the universe! for though the world is so old, and so many books have been written, each object appears wholly undescribed to our experience, each field of thought wholly unexplored. The whole world is an America, a *New World*.

APRIL 4

JOURNAL (APRIL 4, 1840)

We look to windward for fair weather.

APRIL 5

JOURNAL (APRIL 4, 1853)

Rain, rain. . . . The lichens remember the sea to-day. The usually dry cladonias, which are so crisp under the feet, are full of moist vigor. The rocks speak and tell the tales inscribed on them. Their inscriptions are brought out. I pause to study their geography.

APRIL 6

JOURNAL (APRIL 6, 1856)

It is remarkable how large a mansion of the air you can explore with your ears in the still morning by the waterside.

APRIL 7

JOURNAL (APRIL 7, 1853)

If you make the least correct observation of nature this year, you will have occasion to repeat it with

illustrations the next, and the season and life itself is prolonged.

APRIL 8

"ECONOMY," *WALDEN* (1854)

Nature and human life are as various as our several constitutions. Who shall say what prospect life offers to another? Could a greater miracle take place than for us to look through each other's eyes for an instant?

APRIL 9

"LIFE WITHOUT PRINCIPLE" (1863)

In some lyceums they tell me that they have voted to exclude the subject of religion. But how do I know what their religion is, and when I am near to or far from it? I have walked into such an arena and done my best to make a clean breast of what religion I have experienced, and the audience never suspected what I was about. The lecture was as harmless as moonshine to them. [LYCEUMS WERE TOWN-SPONSORED PUBLIC LECTURES.]

APRIL 10

Perhaps on that spring morning when Adam and Eve were driven out of Eden Walden Pond was already in existence, and even then breaking up in a gentle spring rain accompanied with mist and a southerly wind, and covered with myriads of ducks and geese, which had not heard of the fall, when still such pure lakes sufficed them.

APRIL 11

"LIFE WITHOUT PRINCIPLE" (1863)

You cannot serve two masters. It requires more than a day's devotion to know and to possess the wealth of a day.

APRIL 12

JOURNAL (APRIL 12, 1854)

I observe that it is when I have been intently, and it may be laboriously, at work, and am somewhat listless or abandoned after it, reposing, that the muse visits me, and I see or hear beauty. It is from out the shadow of my toil that I look into the light.

APRIL 13

A driving snow-storm in the night and still raging; five or six inches deep on a level at 7 a.m. All birds are turned into snowbirds. . . . But it is good now to stay in the house and read and write. . . . The imprisoning storm condenses our thoughts. I can hear the clock tick as not in pleasant weather. My life is enriched. I love to hear the wind howl.

APRIL 14

If it is asserted that civilization is a real advance in the condition of man,—and I think that it is, though only the wise improve their advantages,—it must be shown that it has produced better dwellings without making them more costly; and the cost of a thing is the amount of what I will call life which is required to be exchanged for it, immediately or in the long run.

APRIL 15

To see a sucker [fish] tossing on the spring flood, its swelling, imbricated breast heaving up a bait to

not-despairing gulls! It is a strong and a strength-ening sight. Is the world coming to an end? Ask the chubs. As long as fishes spawn, glory and honor to the cold-blooded who despair! As long as ideas are expressed, as long as friction makes bright, as long as vibrating wires make music of harps, we do not want [lack] redeemers.

APRIL 16
"CONCLUSION," *WALDEN* (1854)

The life in us is like the water in the river. It may rise this year higher than man has ever known it, and flood the parched uplands; even this may be the eventful year, which will drown out all our muskrats.

APRIL 17
JOURNAL (APRIL 15, 1852)

They [the seagulls] come annually a-fishing here like royal hunters, to remind us of the sea and that our town, after all, lies but further up a creek of the uni-versal sea, above the head of the tide. So ready is a deluge to overwhelm our lands, as the gulls to cir-cle hither in the spring freshets. To see a gull beat-ing high over our meadowy flood in chill and windy March is akin to seeing a mackerel schooner on the

coast. It is the nearest approach to sailing vessels in our scenery. . . . We are so far maritime, do not dwell beyond the range of the seagoing gull, the littoral birds.

APRIL 18
JOURNAL (APRIL 18, 1852)

Why should just these sights and sounds accompany our life? Why should I hear the chattering of blackbirds, why smell the skunk each year? I would fain explore the mysterious relation between myself and these things. I would at least know what these things unavoidably are, make a chart of our life, know how its shores trend, that butterflies reappear and when, know why just this circle of creatures completes the world.

APRIL 19
JOURNAL (APRIL 19, 1852)

To see the larger and wilder birds, you must go forth in the great storms like this. At such times they frequent our neighborhood and trust themselves in our midst. . . . When the storm increases, then these great birds that carry the mail of the seasons lay to. To see wild life you must go forth at a wild season.

APRIL 20

JOURNAL (APRIL 21, 1852)

I am glad that men are so dispersed over the earth. The need of fuel causes woods to be left, and the use of cattle and horses requires pastures, and hence men live far apart and the walkers of every town have this wide range over forest and field.

APRIL 21

JOURNAL (APRIL 21, 1852)

On the east side of Ponkawtasset I hear a robin singing cheerily from some perch in the wood, in the midst of the rain, where the scenery is now wild and dreary. His song a singular antagonism and offset to the storm. As if Nature said, "Have faith, these *two* things I can do."

APRIL 22

"READING," *WALDEN* (1854)

A written word is the choicest of relics. It is something at once more intimate with us and more universal than any other work of art. It is the work of art nearest to life itself. It may be translated into every language, and not only be read but actually breathed from all human lips;—not be represented

on canvas or in marble only, but be carved out of the breath of life itself.

APRIL 23
JOURNAL (JUNE 23, 1840)

We Yankees are not so far from right, who answer one question by asking another. Yes and No are lies. A true answer will not aim to establish anything, but rather to set all well afloat.

APRIL 24
"ECONOMY," WALDEN (1854)

Only they who go to soirées and legislative halls must have new coats, coats to change as often as the man changes in them. But if my jacket and trousers, my hat and shoes, are fit to worship God in, they will do; will they not? . . . I say, beware of all enterprises that require new clothes.

APRIL 25
JOURNAL (APRIL 25, 1854)

The first partridge drums in one or two places, as if the earth's pulse now beat audibly with the increased flow of life. It slightly flutters all Nature and makes

her heart palpitate. Also, as I stand listening for the wren, and sweltering in my greatcoat, I hear the woods filled with the hum of insects, as if my hearing were affected; and thus the summer's quire begins. The silent spaces have begun to be filled.

APRIL 26
"CONCLUSION," *WALDEN* (1854)

Why should we be in such desperate haste to succeed and in such desperate enterprises? If a man does not keep pace with his companions, perhaps it is because he hears a different drummer. Let him step to the music which he hears, however measured or far away. It is not important that he should mature as soon as an apple tree or an oak. Shall he turn his spring into summer?

APRIL 27
JOURNAL (APRIL 17, 1852)

In that little pasture of Potter's under the oak, I am struck with the advantage of the fence in landscapes. Here is but a half-acre inclosed, but the fence has the effect of confining the attention to this little undulation of the land and to make you consider it by itself, and the importance of the oak is proportionally increased. This formation of the surface would

be lost in an unfenced prairie, but the fence, which nearly enough defines it, frames it and presents it as a picture.

APRIL 28
JOURNAL (APRIL 28, 1856)

I [am] reminded of the advantage to the poet, and philosopher, and naturalist, and whomsoever, of pursuing from time to time some other business than his chosen one,—seeing with the side of the eye. The poet will so get visions which no deliberate abandonment can secure. The philosopher is so forced to recognize principles which long study might not detect. And the naturalist even will stumble upon some new and unexpected flower or animal.

APRIL 29
JOURNAL (APRIL 29, 1852)

The art of life, of a poet's life, is, not having anything to do, to do something.

Cattle begin to go up-country. . . . Now many a farm-er's boy makes his first journey, and sees something to tell of,—makes acquaintance with those hills which are mere blue warts in his horizon, finds them solid and *terra firma*, after all, and inhabited by herdsmen, partially befenced and measurable by the acre, with cool springs where you may quench your thirst after a dusty day's walk.

MAY

At length, in the beginning of May, with the help of some of my acquaintances, rather to improve so good an occasion for neighborliness than from any necessity, I set up the frame of my house. No man was ever more honored in the character of his raisers than I. They are destined, I trust, to assist at the raising of loftier structures one day. . . . It would be worth the while to build still more deliberately than I did, considering, for instance, what foundation a door, a window, a cellar, a garret, have in the nature of man. . . . There is some of the same fitness in a man's building his own house that there is in a bird's building its own nest.

"Economy," *Walden* (1854)

෴

MAY 1

It is foolish for a man to accumulate material wealth chiefly, houses and land. Our stock in life, our real estate, is that amount of thought which we have had, which we have thought out.... If you have ever done any work with these finest tools, the imagination and fancy and reason, it is a new creation, independent on the world, and a possession forever.

MAY 2

It appears to me that, to one standing on the heights of philosophy, mankind and the works of man will have sunk out of sight altogether; that man is altogether too much insisted on.... Man is but the place where I stand, and the prospect hence is infinite. It is not a chamber of mirrors which reflect me. When I reflect, I find that there is other than me.

MAY 3

Frogs are the birds of the night.
I go along the side of Fair Haven Hill. The clock

strikes distinctly, showing the wind is easterly. There is a grand, rich, musical echo trembling on the air long after the clock has ceased to strike, like a vast organ, filling the air with a trembling music like a flower of sound.

MAY 4
"ECONOMY," *WALDEN* (1854)

To anticipate, not the sunrise and the dawn merely, but, if possible, Nature herself! How many mornings, summer and winter, before yet any neighbor was stirring about his business, have I been about mine! . . . It is true, I never assisted the sun materially in his rising, but, doubt not, it was of the last importance only to be present at it.

MAY 5
"ECONOMY," *WALDEN* (1854)

The greater part of what my neighbors call good I believe in my soul to be bad, and if I repent of anything, it is very likely to be my good behavior. What demon possessed me that I behaved so well?

MAY 6

There is no such thing as pure *objective* observation. Your observation, to be interesting, *i.e.* to be significant, must be *subjective*. The sum of what the writer of whatever class has to report is simply some human experience, whether he be poet or philosopher or man of science.

MAY 7

Most revolutions in society have not power to interest, still less alarm us, but tell me that our rivers are drying up, or the genus pine dying out in the country, and I might attend. . . . Revolutions are never sudden. The most important is commonly some silent and unobtrusive fact in history.

MAY 8

A field of water betrays the spirit that is in the air. It is continually receiving new life and motion from above. It is intermediate in its nature between land and sky. On land only the grass and trees wave, but the water itself is rippled by the wind. I see where

the breeze dashes across it by the streaks or flakes of light.

MAY 9

JOURNAL (MAY 10, 1854)

In Boston yesterday an ornithologist said significantly, "If you held the bird in your hand—;" but I would rather hold it in my affections.

MAY 10

JOURNAL (MAY 10, 1853)

He is the richest who has most use for nature as raw material of tropes and symbols with which to describe his life. If these gates of golden willows affect me, they correspond to the beauty and promise of some experience on which I am entering. If I am overflowing with life, am rich in experience for which I lack expression, then nature will be my language full of poetry,—all nature will *fable*, and every natural phenomenon be a myth.

MAY 11
JOURNAL (MAY 11, 1853)

How many little birds of the warbler family are busy now about the opening buds, while I sit by the spring! They are almost as much a part of the tree as its blossoms and leaves. They come and give it voice.

MAY 12
JOURNAL (MAY 12, 1850)

Nothing memorable was ever accomplished in a prosaic mood of mind. The heroes and discoverers have found true more than was previously believed, only when they were expecting and dreaming of something more than their contemporaries dreamed of,—when they were in a frame of mind prepared in some measure for the truth.

MAY 13
JOURNAL (MAY 13, 1852)

All these expanding leaves and flower-buds are much more beautiful in the rain,—covered with clear drops. They have lost some of their beauty when I have shaken the drops off. They who do not walk in the woods in the rain never behold them in their freshest, most radiant and blooming beauty.

MAY 14

JOURNAL (MAY 13, 1860)

I observe this morning the dew on the grass in our yard,—literally sparkling drops, which thickly stud it. Each dewdrop is a beautiful crystalline sphere just below (within an eighth of an inch more or less) the tip of the blade. Sometimes there are two or three, one beneath the other, the lowest the largest. Each dewdrop takes the form of the planet itself. . . . The surface of the globe is thus tremblingly alive.

MAY 15

JOURNAL (MAY 15, 1853)

The first cricket's chirrup which I have chanced to hear now falls on my ear and makes me forget all else. . . . His voice has set me thinking, philosophizing, moralizing at once. It is not so wildly melodious, but it is wiser and more mature than that of the wood thrush. With this elixir I see clear through the summer now to autumn, and any summer work seems frivolous.

MAY 16

JOURNAL (MAY 1850)

I have noticed the effect of a flag set up on a hill in

the country. It tames the landscape, subdues it to itself. The hill looks as if it were a military post. Our green, wild country landscape is gathered under the folds of a flag.

MAY 17

JOURNAL (MAY 17, 1854)

Observed a rill [small stream] emptying in above the stone-heaps, and afterward saw where it ran out of June-Berry Meadow, and I considered how surely it would have conducted me to the meadow, if I had traced it up. I was impressed as it were by the intelligence of the brook, which for ages in the wildest regions, before science is born, knows so well the level of the ground, and through whatever woods or other obstacles finds its way. Who shall distinguish between the *law* by which a brook finds its river, the *instinct* [by which] a bird performs its migrations, and the *knowledge* by which a man steers his ship round the globe?

MAY 18

*A WEEK ON THE CONCORD AND
MERRIMACK RIVERS* (1849)

Your scheme must be the framework of the universe; all other schemes will soon be ruins.

MAY 19

I have found repeatedly, of late years, that I cannot fish without falling a little in self-respect. I have tried it again and again. I have skill at it, and, like many of my fellows, a certain instinct for it, which revives from time to time, but always when I have done I feel that it would have been better if I had not fished.

MAY 20

The ocean is a wilderness reaching round the globe, wilder than a Bengal jungle, and fuller of monsters, washing the very wharves of our cities and the gardens of our sea-side residences. Serpents, bears, hyenas, tigers, rapidly vanish as civilization advances, but the most populous and civilized city cannot scare a shark far from its wharves.

MAY 21

Once it chanced that I stood in the very abutment of a rainbow's arch, which filled the lower stratum of the atmosphere, tinging the grass and leaves around,

and dazzling me as if I looked through colored crystal. It was a lake of rainbow light, in which, for a short while, I lived like a dolphin. If it had lasted longer it might have tinged my employments and life.

MAY 22
JOURNAL (MAY 22, 1854)

First observe the creak of crickets. . . . To the birds they say: "Ah! you speak like children from impulse; Nature speaks through you; but with us it is ripe knowledge. The seasons do not revolve for us; we sing their lullaby." So they chant, eternal, at the roots of the grass.

MAY 23
"THE BEAN-FIELD," *WALDEN* (1854)

The nighthawk circled overhead in the sunny afternoons—for I sometimes made a day of it—like a mote in the eye, or in heaven's eye, falling from time to time with a swoop and a sound as if the heavens were rent . . . graceful and slender like ripples caught up from the pond, as leaves are raised by the wind to float in the heavens; such kindredship is in nature. The hawk is aerial brother of the wave which he sails over and surveys, those his perfect air-inflated wings

answering to the elemental unfledged pinions of the sea.

MAY 24
"CONCLUSION," *WALDEN* (1854)

I fear chiefly lest my expression may not be *extra-vagant* enough, may not wander far enough beyond the narrow limits of my daily experience, so as to be adequate to the truth of which I have been convinced. *Extra vagance!* it depends on how you are yarded.

MAY 25
A WEEK ON THE CONCORD AND MERRIMACK RIVERS (1849)

I would give all the wealth of the world, and all the deeds of all the heroes, for one true vision. But how can I communicate with the gods, who am a pencil-maker on the earth, and not be insane?

MAY 26
JOURNAL (1837–47)

A state should be a complete epitome of the earth, a natural principality, and by the gradations of its

surface and soil conduct the traveller to its principal marts. Nature is stronger than law, and the sure but slow influence of wind and water will balk the efforts of restricting legislatures. Man cannot set up bounds with safety but where the revolutions of nature will confirm and strengthen, not obliterate, them.

MAY 27

"CIVIL DISOBEDIENCE" (1849)

Thus the State never intentionally confronts a man's sense, intellectual or moral, but only his body, his senses. It is not armed with superior wit or honesty, but with superior physical strength. I was not born to be forced. I will breathe after my own fashion. Let us see who is the strongest. What force has a multitude? They only can force me who obey a higher law than I.

MAY 28

JOURNAL (MAY 28, 1854)

It would be worth the while to ask ourselves weekly, Is our life innocent enough? Do we live *inhumanely*, toward man or beast, in thought or act? To be serene and successful we must be at one with the universe. The least conscious and needless injury inflicted on any creature is to its extent a suicide.

I see the Court-House full of armed men, holding prisoner and trying a MAN, to find out if he is not really a SLAVE. It is a question about which there is great doubt.

It is really the trial of Massachusetts. Every moment that she hesitates to set this man free, she is convicted. The Commissioner on her case is God. . . . Rather than thus consent to establish hell upon earth,—to be a party to this establishment,—I would touch a match to blow up earth and hell together.

[REACTING TO THE BOSTON TRIAL OF ANTHONY BURNS, WHO HAD ESCAPED SLAVERY AND WAS THEN ARRESTED AND RE-TURNED TO HIS VIRGINIA SLAVEHOLDER BY THE FEDERAL GOVERNMENT.]

MAY 30

"READING," *WALDEN* (1854)

There are probably words addressed to our condition exactly, which, if we could really hear and understand, would be more salutary than the morning or the spring to our lives How many a man has dated a new era in his life from the reading of a book.

We notice that it required a separate intention of
the eye, a more free and abstracted vision, to see the
reflected trees and the sky, than to see the river bot-
tom merely; and so are there manifold visions in the
direction of every object, and even the most opaque
reflect the heavens from their surface.

JUNE

Life consists with wildness. The most alive is the wildest. Not yet subdued to man, its presence refreshes him. One who pressed forward incessantly and never rested from his labors, who grew fast and made infinite demands on life, would always find himself in a new country or wilderness, and surrounded by the raw material of life. . . . Hope and the future for me are not in lawns and cultivated fields, not in towns and cities, but in the impervious and quaking swamps.

"Walking" (1862)

JUNE 1
"SOLITUDE," *WALDEN* (1854)

The gentle rain which waters my beans and keeps
me in the house to-day is not drear and melancholy,
but good for me too. Though it prevents my hoe-
ing them, it is of far more worth than my hoeing.
If it should continue so long as to cause the seeds
to rot in the ground and destroy the potatoes in the
low lands, it would still be good for the grass on the
uplands, and, being good for the grass, it would be
good for me.

JUNE 2
"WALKING" (1862)

We should go forth on the shortest walk, perchance,
in the spirit of undying adventure, never to return,—
prepared to send back our embalmed hearts only
as relics to our desolate kingdoms. If you are ready
to leave father and mother, and brother and sister,
and wife and child and friends, and never see them
again,—if you have paid your debts, and made your
will, and settled all your affairs, and are a free man,
then you are ready for a walk.

JUNE 3

*A WEEK ON THE CONCORD AND
MERRIMACK RIVERS* (1849)

There is a chasm between knowledge and ignorance
which the arches of science can never span. . . . We
do not learn much from learned books, but from
true, sincere, human books, from frank and honest
biographies.

JUNE 4

JOURNAL (JUNE 4, 1860)

One asks me to-day when it is that the leaves are
fully expanded, so that the trees and woods look dark
and heavy with leaves. . . . Each tree (or most trees)
now holds out many little twigs, some three inches
long, with two or three fully expanded leaves on it,
between us and the sun, making already a grateful
but thin shade, like a coarse sieve, so open that we
see the fluttering of each leaf in its shadow; but in a
week or more the twigs will have so extended them-
selves, and the number of fully expanded leaves be
so increased, that the trees will look heavy and dark
with foliage and the shadow be dark and opaque,—a
gelid shade.

JUNE 5

JOURNAL (JUNE 5, 1857)

I am interested in each contemporary plant in my vicinity, and have attained to a certain acquaintance with the larger ones. They are cohabitants with me of this part of the planet, and they bear familiar names. Yet how essentially wild they are! as wild, really, as those strange fossil plants whose impressions I see on my coal. . . . Chick-weed, or a pine tree, is but little less wild. I assume to be acquainted with these, but what ages between me and the tree whose shade I enjoy! It is as if it stood substantially in a remote geological period.

JUNE 6

JOURNAL (JUNE 6, 1857)

This is June, the month of grass and leaves. . . . I feel a little fluttered in my thoughts, as if I might be too late. Each season is but an infinitesimal point. It no sooner comes than it is gone. . . . Our thoughts and sentiments answer to the revolutions of the seasons, as two cog-wheels fit into each other. We are conversant with only one point of contact at a time, from which we receive a prompting and impulse and instantly pass to a new season or point of contact. . . . Now I am ice, now I am sorrel.

JUNE 7

JOURNAL (JUNE 5, 1852)

The lupine is now in its glory. . . . The earth is blued with them. . . . You passed along here, perchance, a fortnight ago, and the hillside was comparatively barren, but now you come and these glorious redeemers appear to have flashed out here all at once. Who planted the seeds of lupines in the barren soil? Who watereth the lupines in the fields?

JUNE 8

JOURNAL (JUNE 16, 1840)

So is not shade as good as sunshine, night as day? Why be eagles and thrushes always, and owls and whip-poor-wills never?

JUNE 9

"VISITORS," *WALDEN* (1854)

Girls and boys and young women generally seemed glad to be in the woods. They looked in the pond and at the flowers, and improved their time. Men of business, even farmers, thought only of solitude and employment, and of the great distance at which I dwelt from something or other; and though they

said that they loved a ramble in the woods occasion-
ally, it was obvious that they did not.

JUNE 10
JOURNAL (JUNE 11, 1855)

What if we feel a yearning to which no breast answers?
I walk alone. My heart is full. Feelings impede the
current of my thoughts. I knock on the earth for my
friend. I expect to meet him at every turn; but no
friend appears. . . . I would fain walk on the deep
waters, but my companions will only walk on shal-
lows and puddles.

JUNE 11
JOURNAL (JUNE 11, 1851)

No one, to my knowledge, has observed the min-
ute differences in the seasons. Hardly two nights are
alike. The rocks do not feel warm to-night, for the air
is warmest; nor does the sand particularly. A book of
the seasons, each page of which should be written
in its own season and out-of-doors.

JUNE 12

JOURNAL (JUNE 12, 1852)

Boys are bathing at Hubbard's Bend, playing with a boat. . . . The color of their bodies in the sun at a distance is pleasing, the not often seen flesh-color. I hear the sound of their sport borne over the water. . . . What a singular fact for an angel visitant to this earth to carry back in his note-book, that men were forbidden to expose their bodies under the severest penalties!

JUNE 13

"ECONOMY," *WALDEN* (1854)

Public opinion is a weak tyrant compared with our own private opinion. What a man thinks of himself, that it is which determines, or rather indicates, his fate.

JUNE 14

JOURNAL (JUNE 15, 1852)

Do not hire a man who does your work for money, but him who does it for love, and pay him well.

JUNE 15

JOURNAL (JUNE 16, 1854)

Again I scent the white water-lily, and a season I had waited for is arrived. . . . What confirmation of our hopes is in the fragrance of the water-lily! I shall not so soon despair of the world for it, notwithstanding slavery, and the cowardice and want of principle of the North. It suggests that the time may come when man's deeds will smell as sweet.

JUNE 16

JOURNAL (JUNE 16, 1854)

There is a fine ripple and sparkle on the pond, seen through the mist. But what signifies the beauty of nature when men are base? We walk to lakes to see our serenity reflected in them. When we are not serene, we go not to them. Who can be serene in a country where both rulers and ruled are without principle? The remembrance of the baseness of politicians spoils my walks. My thoughts are murder to the State. [AFTER THE RENDITION OF ANTHONY BURNS TO SLAVERY.]

JUNE 17
JOURNAL (JUNE 17, 1854)

The season of hope and promise is past; already the season of small fruits has arrived. The Indian marked the midsummer as the season when berries were ripe. We are a little saddened, because we begin to see the interval between our hopes and their fulfillment.

JUNE 18
JOURNAL (JUNE 18, 1860)

The tumultuous singing of birds, a burst of melody, wakes me up (the window being open) these mornings at dawn. What a *matinade* to have poured into your slumber!

JUNE 19
JOURNAL (JUNE 18, 1853)

Moon not quite full. . . . How can a man write the same thoughts by the light of the moon, resting his book on a rail by the side of a remote potato-field, that he does by the light of the sun, on his study table? The light is but a luminousness. My pencil seems to move through a creamy, mystic medium.

JUNE 20

JOURNAL (JUNE 20, 1852)

Lying with my window open, these warm, even sultry nights, I hear the sonorously musical trump of the bullfrogs from time to time, from some distant shore of the river, as if the world were given up to them. By those villagers who live on the street they are never seen and rarely heard by day, but in the quiet sultry nights their notes ring from one end of the town to another. It is as if you had waked up in the infernal regions. I do not know for a time in what world I am.

JUNE 21

JOURNAL (JUNE 21, 1852)

Nature has looked uncommonly bare and dry to me for a day or two. With our senses applied to the surrounding world we are reading our own physical and corresponding moral revolutions. Nature was so shallow all at once I did not know what had attracted me all my life. I was therefore encouraged when, going through a field this evening, I was unexpectedly struck with the beauty of an apple tree.

JUNE 22

As I come over the hill, I hear the wood thrush sing-
ing his evening lay. This is the only bird whose note
affects me like music, affects the flow and tenor of
my thought, my fancy and imagination. . . . I long
for wildness, a nature which I cannot put my foot
through, woods where the wood thrush forever
sings, where the hours are early morning ones, and
there is dew on the grass, and the day is forever
unproved, where I might have a fertile unknown for
a soil about me.

JUNE 23

A skunk-cabbage leaf makes the best vessel to drink
out of at a spring. It is so large, already somewhat
dishing, oftenest entire, and grows near at hand,
and, though its odor where the stem is cut off is
offensive, it does not flavor the water and is not per-
ceived in drinking.

JUNE 24

JOURNAL (JUNE 19, 1852)

Facts collected by a poet are set down at last as winged seeds of truth, samarae, tinged with his expectation. Oh, may my words be verdurous and sempiternal as the hills! Facts fall from the poetic observer as ripe seeds.

JUNE 25

JOURNAL (JUNE 23, 1840)

He is the true artist whose life is his material; every stroke of the chisel must enter his own flesh and bone and not grate dully on marble.

JUNE 26

JOURNAL (JUNE 26, 1840)

When a dog runs at you, whistle for him.

JUNE 27

As we thus dipped our way along between fresh masses of foliage overrun with the grape and smaller flowering vines, the surface was so calm, and both air and water so transparent, that the flight of a kingfisher or robin over the river was as distinctly seen reflected in the water below as in the air above. The birds seemed to flit through submerged groves, alighting on the yielding sprays, and their clear notes to come up from below. We were uncertain whether the water floated the land, or the land held the water in its bosom.

JUNE 28

Every morning was a cheerful invitation to make my life of equal simplicity, and I may say innocence, with Nature herself. I have been as sincere a worshipper of Aurora as the Greeks. I got up early and bathed in the pond; that was a religious exercise, and one of the best things which I did.

JUNE 29

*A WEEK ON THE CONCORD AND
MERRIMACK RIVERS* (1849)

Read the best books first, or you may not have a
chance to read them at all.

JUNE 30

JOURNAL (JUNE 30, 1852)

Nature must be viewed humanly to be viewed at all;
that is, her scenes must be associated with humane
affections, such as are associated with one's native
place, for instance. She is most significant to a lover.
A lover of Nature is preëminently a lover of man. If I
have no friend, what is Nature to me? She ceases to
be morally significant.

JULY

Time is but the stream I go a-fishing in. I drink at it; but while I drink I see the sandy bottom and detect how shallow it is. Its thin current slides away, but eternity remains. I would drink deeper; fish in the sky, whose bottom is pebbly with stars. I cannot count one. I know not the first letter of the alphabet. I have always been regretting that I was not as wise as the day I was born. The intellect is a cleaver; it discerns and rifts its way into the secret of things. I do not wish to be any more busy with my hands than is necessary. My head is hands and feet. I feel all my best faculties concentrated in it. My instinct tells me that my head is an organ for burrowing, as some creatures use their snout and fore paws, and with it I would mine and burrow my way through these hills. I think that the richest vein is somewhere hereabouts; so by the divining rod and thin rising vapors I judge; and here I will begin to mine.

"Where I Lived, and What
I Lived For," *Walden* (1854)

JULY 1

To him whose elastic and vigorous thought keeps
pace with the sun, the day is a perpetual morning.
It matters not what the clocks say or the attitudes
and labors of men. Morning is when I am awake and
there is a dawn in me.

JULY 2

JOURNAL (JULY 6, 1840)

Let the daily tide leave some deposit on these pages,
as it leaves sand and shells on the shore. So much
increase of *terra firma*. This may be a calendar of the
ebbs and flows of the soul; and on these sheets as a
beach, the waves may cast up pearls and seaweed.

JULY 3

JOURNAL (JULY 3, 1854)

What a luxury to bathe now! It is gloriously hot,—the
first of this weather. I cannot get wet enough. I must
let the water soak into me. When you come out, it
is rapidly dried on you or absorbed into your body,
and you want to go in again.

JULY 4

When first I took up my abode in the woods, that is, began to spend my nights as well as days there, which, by accident, was on Independence Day, or the Fourth of July, 1845, my house was not finished for winter, but was merely a defense against the rain. . . . The winds which passed over my dwelling were such as sweep over the ridges of mountains, bearing the broken strains, or celestial parts only, of terrestrial music. The morning wind forever blows, the poem of creation is uninterrupted; but few are the ears that hear it.

JULY 5

I love to ponder the natural history thus written on the banks of the stream, for every higher freshet [stream] and intenser frost is recorded by it. The stream keeps a faithful and a true journal of every event in its experience, whatever race may settle on its banks; and it purls past this natural graveyard with a storied murmur, and no doubt it could find endless employment for an old mortality in renewing its epitaphs.

JULY 6

JOURNAL (JULY 6, 1852)

The early blueberries ripen first on the hills, before those who confine themselves to the lowlands are aware of it. When the old folks find only one turned here and there, children, who are best acquainted with the localities of berries, bring pailfuls to sell at their doors. For birds' nests and berries, give me a child's eyes.

JULY 7

JOURNAL (JULY 7, 1852)

4 a.m.—The first really foggy morning. Yet before I rise I hear the song of birds from out it, like the bursting of its bubbles with music, the bead on liquids just uncorked. Their song gilds thus the frostwork of the morning. As if the fog were a great sweet froth on the surface of land and water, whose fixed air escaped, whose bubbles burst with music. . . . Sleep with all your windows open, and let the mist embrace you.

JULY 8

JOURNAL (JULY 6, 1851)

There is some advantage in being the humblest, cheapest, least dignified man in the village, so that

the very stable boys shall damn you. Methinks I enjoy
that advantage to an unusual extent.

JULY 9

"ECONOMY," *WALDEN* (1854)

I had three pieces of limestone on my desk, but I was
terrified to find that they required to be dusted daily,
when the furniture of my mind was all undusted still,
and I threw them out the window in disgust. How,
then, could I have a furnished house? I would rather
sit in the open air, for no dust gathers on the grass,
unless where man has broken ground.

JULY 10

JOURNAL (JULY 10, 1851)

I am always struck by the centrality of the observer's
position. He always stands fronting the middle of the
arch, and does not suspect at first that a thousand
observers on a thousand hills behold the sunset sky
from equally favorable positions.

JULY 11
JOURNAL (JULY 11, 1852)

What is called genius is the abundance of life or health, so that whatever addresses the senses, as the flavor of these berries, or the lowing of that cow... each sight and sound and scent and flavor,— intoxicates with a healthy intoxication. . . . I am thrilled to think that I owe a perception to the commonly gross sense of taste, that I have been inspired through the palate, that these berries have fed my brain.

JULY 12
"CONCLUSION," *WALDEN* (1854)

What youthful philosophers and experimentalists we are! There is not one of my readers who has yet lived a whole human life. These may be but the spring months in the life of the race.

[JULY 12 WAS THOREAU'S BIRTHDAY.]

JULY 13
JOURNAL* (1842–44)

Why should the present impose upon us so much! I sit now upon a stump whose rings number centuries of growth—If I look around me I see that the very

soil is composed of just such stumps—ancestors to this. I thrust this stick many aeons deep into the surface—and with my heel scratch a deeper furrow than the elements have ploughed here for a thousand years—If I listen I hear the peep of frogs which is older than the slime of Egypt—or a distant partridge drumming on a log—as if it were the pulse-beat of the summer air.

JULY 14

"WINTER ANIMALS," *WALDEN* (1854)

I once had a sparrow alight upon my shoulder for a moment while I was hoeing in a village garden, and I felt that I was more distinguished by that circumstance than I should have been by any epaulet I could have worn.

JULY 15

JOURNAL (JULY 16, 1851)

Methinks this is the first of dog-days. The air in the distance has a peculiar blue mistiness, or furnace-like look, though, as I have said, it is not sultry yet. It is not the season for distant views. . . . The air is the opposite to what it is in October and November. You are not inclined to travel. It is a world of orchards and small-fruits now, and you can stay at home if the well has cool water in it.

JULY 16

Berries are just beginning to ripen, and children are planning expeditions after them. They are important as introducing children to the fields and woods, and as wild fruits of which much account is made. . . . I remember how glad I was when I was kept from school a half a day to pick huckleberries on a neighboring hill all by myself to make a pudding for the family dinner. Ah, they got nothing but the pudding, but I got invaluable experience beside! A half a day of liberty like that was like the promise of life eternal.

JULY 17

I think that no experience which I have to-day comes up to, or is comparable with, the experiences of my boyhood. . . . For years I marched as to a music in comparison with which the military music of the streets is noise and discord. I was daily intoxicated, and yet no man could call me intemperate. With all your science can you tell how it is, and whence it is, that light comes into the soul?

JULY 18

When I think of the London *Times* and the reviews here, the *Revue des Deux Mondes*, and of the kind of life which it is possible to live here, I perceive that this, the natural side, has not got into literature. Think of an essay on human life, through all which was heard the note of the huckleberry-bird still ringing, as here it rings ceaselessly. . . . The *Revue des Deux Mondes* does not embrace this view of things, nor imply it.

JULY 19

"CONCLUSION," *WALDEN* (1854)

The fault-finder will find faults even in paradise.

JULY 20

"A WALK TO WACHUSETT" (1843)

The night was, in its elements, simple even to majesty in that bleak place,—a bright moonlight and a piercing wind. It was at no time darker than twilight within the tent, and we could easily see the moon through its transparent roof as we lay; for there was the moon still above us, with Jupiter and Saturn on either hand, looking down on Wachusett,

and it was a satisfaction to know that they were our fellow-travelers still, as high and out of our reach as our own destiny.

[THOREAU WALKED TO MOUNT WACHUSETT ON JULY 19–20, 1842, WITH MARGARET FULLER'S BROTHER RICHARD.]

JULY 21
JOURNAL (JULY 21, 1851)

8:30 p.m.—The streets of the village are much more interesting to me at this hour of a summer evening than by day. Neighbors, and also farmers, come a-shopping after their day's haying, are chatting in the streets, and I hear the sound of many musical instruments and of singing from various houses. For a short hour or two the inhabitants are sensibly employed. The evening is devoted to poetry, such as the villagers can appreciate.

JULY 22
JOURNAL (JULY 22, 1851)

The season of morning fogs has arrived. I think it is connected with dog-days. Perhaps it is owing to the greater contrast between the night and the day, the nights being nearly as cold, while the days are warmer? Before I rise from my couch, I see the ambrosial fog stretched over the river, draping

the trees. . . . It is almost musical; it is positively fragrant.

JULY 23
"THE VILLAGE," *WALDEN* (1854)

One afternoon, near the end of the first summer, when I went to the village to get a shoe from the cobbler's, I was seized and put into jail, because, as I have elsewhere related, I did not pay a tax to, or recognize the authority of, the State which buys and sells men, women, and children, like cattle at the door of its senate-house. I had gone down to the woods for other purposes. But, wherever a man goes, men will pursue and paw him with their dirty institutions. [THOREAU WAS JAILED FOR NONPAYMENT OF TAXES ON JULY 23, 1846.]

JULY 24
JOURNAL* (JULY 24, 1846)

In my short experience of human life I have found that the outward obstacles which stood in my way were not living men—but dead institutions. . . . If I will not fight—if I will not pray—if I will not be taxed—if I will not bury the unsettled prairie—my neighbor will still tolerate me and sometimes even sustains me—but not the state.

[AFTER THOREAU WAS RELEASED FROM JAIL.]

JULY 25

I was put into jail as I was going to the shoemaker's to get a shoe which was mended. When I was let out the next morning, I proceeded to finish my errand, and, having put on my mended shoe, joined a huckleberry party, who were impatient to put themselves under my conduct; and in half an hour,—for the horse was soon tackled,—was in the midst of a huckleberry field, on one of our highest hills, two miles off, and then the State was nowhere to be seen.

JULY 26

Wines of all kinds and qualities, of noblest vintages, are bottled up in the skins of countless berries, for the taste of men and animals. To men they seem offered not so much for food as for sociality, that they may picnic with Nature,—diet drinks, cordials, wines. We pluck and eat in remembrance of Her. It is a sacrament, a communion. The not-forbidden fruits, which no serpent tempts us to taste.

Spring is the reign of water; summer, of heat and dryness; winter, of cold. Whole families of plants that lately flourished have disappeared. Now the phenomena are tropical. Let our summer last long enough, and our land would wear the aspect of the tropics.

Methinks the season culminated about the middle of this month,—that the year was of indefinite promise before, but that, after the first intense heats, we postponed the fulfillment of many of our hopes for this year, and, having as it were attained the ridge of the summer, commenced to descend the long slope toward winter, the afternoon and down-hill of the year. Last evening it was much cooler, and I heard a decided fall sound of crickets.

JULY 29

"ECONOMY," *WALDEN* (1854)

In the long run men hit only what they aim at. Therefore, though they should fail immediately, they had better aim at something high.

JULY 30

"CONCLUSION," *WALDEN* (1854)

Give me a hammer, and let me feel for the furrowing. Do not depend on the putty. Drive a nail home and clinch it so faithfully that you can wake up in the night and think of your work with satisfaction,—a work at which you would not be ashamed to invoke the Muse. So will help you God, and so only. Every nail driven should be as another rivet in the machine of the universe, you carrying on the work.

JULY 31

JOURNAL (JULY 27, 1840)

The wood thrush is a more modern philosopher than Plato and Aristotle. They are now a dogma, but he preaches the doctrine of this hour.

AUGUST

When I was four years old, as I well remember, I was brought from Boston to this my native town, through these very woods and this field, to the pond. It is one of the oldest scenes stamped on my memory. And now to-night my flute has waked the echoes over that very water. The pines still stand here older than I; or, if some have fallen, I have cooked my supper with their stumps, and a new growth is rising all around, preparing another aspect for new infant eyes.

"The Bean-Field," *Walden* (1854)

AUGUST 1

"VISITORS," *WALDEN* (1854)

It is surprising how many great men and women a small house will contain.

[ON AUGUST 1, 1846, THOREAU HOSTED A MEETING OF THE CONCORD FEMALE ANTI-SLAVERY SOCIETY AT HIS WALDEN HOUSE.]

AUGUST 2

"SOLITUDE," *WALDEN* (1854)

I have a great deal of company in my house; especially in the morning, when nobody calls. Let me suggest a few comparisons, that some one may convey an idea of my situation. I am no more lonely than the loon in the pond that laughs so loud, or than Walden Pond itself. What company has that lonely lake, I pray? . . . I am no more lonely than a single mullein or dandelion in a pasture, or a bean leaf, or sorrel, or a horse-fly, or a humblebee. I am no more lonely than the Mill Brook, or a weathercock, or the north star, or the south wind, or an April shower, or a January thaw, or the first spider in a new house.

AUGUST 3

JOURNAL (AUGUST 7, 1854)

From this off side of the year, this imbricated slope, with alternating burnished surfaces and shady ledges, much more light and heat is reflected (less absorbed), methinks, than from the springward side. In mid-summer we are of the earth,—confounded with it,—and covered with its dust. Now we begin to erect ourselves somewhat and walk upon its surface. I am not so much reminded of former years, as of existence prior to years.

AUGUST 4

THE MAINE WOODS (1864)

Strange that so few ever come to the woods to see how the pine lives and grows and spires, lifting its evergreen arms to the light,—to see its perfect success; but most are content to behold it in the shape of many broad boards brought to market, and deem *that* its true success! But the pine is no more lumber than man is. . . . A pine cut down, a dead pine, is no more a pine than a dead human carcass is a man. . . . Every creature is better alive than dead, men and moose and pine trees, and he who understands it aright will rather preserve its life than destroy it.

AUGUST 5

JOURNAL (AUGUST 5, 1854)

I find that we are now in the midst of the meadow-haying season, and almost every meadow or section of a meadow has its band of half a dozen mowers and rakers, either bending to their manly work with regular and graceful motion or resting in the shade, while the boys are turning the grass to the sun. I passed as many as sixty or a hundred men thus at work to-day. They stick up a twig with the leaves on, on the river's brink, as a guide for the mowers, that they may not exceed the owner's bounds. I hear their scythes cronching the coarse weeds by the river's brink as I row near.

AUGUST 6

JOURNAL (AUGUST 6, 1858)

I hear of pickers ordered out of the huckleberry-fields, and I see stakes set up with written notices forbidding any to pick there. Some let their fields, or allow so much for the picking. *Sic transit gloria ruris.* We are not grateful enough that we have lived part of our lives before these evil days come. What becomes of the true value of country life? What if you must go to market for it? . . . The wild fruits of the earth disappear before civilization, or are only to be found in large markets. The whole country becomes, as it

were, a town or beaten common, and the fruits left
are a few hips and haws.

AUGUST 7

JOURNAL (AUGUST 7, 1852)

If I were to choose a time for a friend to make a pass-
ing visit to this world for the first time, in the full pos-
session of all his faculties, perchance it would be at a
moment when the sun was setting with splendor in
the west, his light reflected far and wide through the
clarified air after a rain, and a brilliant rainbow, as
now, o'erarching the eastern sky. Would he be likely
to think this a vulgar place to live, where one would
weary of existence, and be compelled to devote his
life to frivolity and dissipation? If a man travelling
from world to world were to pass through this world
at such a moment, would he not be tempted to take
up his abode here?

AUGUST 8

JOURNAL (AUGUST 8, 1851)

To lie here on your back with nothing between your
eye and the stars,—nothing but space,—they your
nearest neighbors on that side, be they strange or
be they tame, be they other worlds or merely orna-

ments to this, who could ever go to sleep under these circumstances? . . . Since I sat here a bright star has gone behind the stem of a tree, proving that my machine is moving,—proving it better for me than a rotating pendulum. I hear a solitary whip-poor-will. . . . And now the star appears on the other side of the tree, and I must go.

AUGUST 9
JOURNAL (AUGUST 9, 1853)

This is the season of small fruits. I trust, too, that I am maturing some small fruit as palatable in these months, which will communicate my flavor to my kind.

AUGUST 10
JOURNAL (AUGUST 8, 1852)

No man ever makes a discovery, ever an observation of the least importance, but he is advertised of the fact by a joy that surprises him. The powers thus celebrate all discovery.

AUGUST 11

It would be well, perhaps, if we were to spend more of our days and nights without any obstruction between us and the celestial bodies, if the poet did not speak so much from under a roof, or the saint dwell there so long. Birds do not sing in caves, nor do doves cherish their innocence in dovecots.

AUGUST 12

The days for some time have been sensibly shorter; there is time for music in the evening.

AUGUST 13

It is a vulgar error to suppose that you have tasted huckleberries who never plucked them. A huckleberry never reaches Boston; they have not been known there since they grew on her three hills. The ambrosial and essential part of the fruit is lost with the bloom which is rubbed off in the market cart, and they become mere provender.

AUGUST 14

Is it not as language that all natural objects affect the poet? He sees a flower or other object, and it is beautiful or affecting to him because it is a symbol of his thought, and what he indistinctly feels or perceives is matured in some other organization. The objects I behold correspond to my mood.

The past has been a remarkably wet week, and now the earth is strewn with fungi. The earth itself is mouldy. . . . Great toadstools stand in the woods.

AUGUST 15

"ECONOMY," *WALDEN* (1854)

How can he remember well his ignorance—which his growth requires—who has so often to use his knowledge?

AUGUST 16

JOURNAL (AUGUST 18, 1853)

The season of flowers or of promise may be said to be over, and now is the season of fruits; but where is our fruit? . . . All nature prompts and reproves us. How early in the year it begins to be late!

AUGUST 17

JOURNAL (AUGUST 17, 1851)

My heart leaps into my mouth at the sound of the wind in the woods. I, whose life was but yesterday so desultory and shallow, suddenly recover my spirits, my spirituality, through my hearing.... Ah! if I could so live that there should be no desultory moment in all my life! that in the trivial season, when small fruits are ripe, my fruits might be ripe also! that I could match nature always with my moods! that in each season when some part of nature especially flourishes, then a corresponding part of me may not fail to flourish!

AUGUST 18

JOURNAL (AUGUST 18, 1841)

I sailed on the North River last night with my flute, and my music was a tinkling stream which meandered with the river, and fell from note to note as a brook from rock to rock. I did not hear the strains after they had issued from the flute, but before they were breathed into it, for the original strain precedes the sound by as much as the echo follows after, and the rest is the perquisite of the rocks and trees and beasts.

AUGUST 19
JOURNAL (AUGUST 19, 1853)

Cooler weather. Last Sunday we were sweltering here and one hundred died of the heat in New York; to-day they have fires in this village. After more rain, with wind in the night, it is now clearing up cool. . . . I was going to sit and write or mope all day in the house, but it seems wise to cultivate animal spirits, to embark in enterprises which employ and recreate the whole body.

AUGUST 20
JOURNAL (AUGUST 20, 1851)

A traveller who looks at things with an impartial eye may see what the oldest inhabitant has not observed.

AUGUST 21
"WHERE I LIVED, AND WHAT I LIVED
FOR," *WALDEN* (1854)

This small lake was of most value as a neighbor in the intervals of a gentle rain-storm in August, when, both air and water being perfectly still, but the sky overcast, mid-afternoon had all the serenity of evening, and the wood thrush sang around, and was heard from shore to shore.

AUGUST 22

JOURNAL (AUGUST 22, 1854)

Walking may be a science, so far as the direction of a walk is concerned. I go again to the Great Meadows, to improve this remarkably dry season and walk where in ordinary times I cannot go. There is, no doubt, a particular season of the year when each place may be visited with most profit and pleasure, and it may be worth the while to consider what that season is in each case.

AUGUST 23

JOURNAL (AUGUST 23, 1853)

Live in each season as it passes; breathe the air, drink the drink, taste the fruit, and resign yourself to the influences of each. . . . For all Nature is doing her best each moment to make us well. She exists for no other end. Do not resist her. . . . Why, "nature" is but another name for health, and the seasons are but different states of health. Some men think that they are not well in spring, or summer, or autumn, or winter; it is only because they are not *well in* them.

AUGUST 24

JOURNAL (AUGUST 24, 1852)

The year is but a succession of days, and I see that I could assign some office to each day which, summed up, would be the history of the year. Everything is done in season, and there is no time to spare. The bird gets its brood hatched in season and is off. I looked into the nest where I saw a vireo feeding its young a few days ago, but it is empty; it is fledged and flown.

AUGUST 25

JOURNAL (AUGUST 23, 1852)

What are these rivers and hills, these hieroglyphics which my eyes behold? There is something invigorating in this air, which I am peculiarly sensible is a real wind, blowing from over the surface of a planet. I look out at my eyes, I come to my window, and I feel and breathe the fresh air. It is a fact equally glorious with the most inward experience.

AUGUST 26

"THE POND IN WINTER," *WALDEN* (1854)

It is remarkable how long men will believe in the bottomlessness of a pond without taking the trouble to

sound it. . . . But I can assure my readers that Walden has a reasonably tight bottom at a not unreasonable, though at an unusual, depth. . . . What if all ponds were shallow? Would it not react on the minds of men? I am thankful that this pond was made deep and pure for a symbol.

AUGUST 27
JOURNAL (AUGUST 24, 1860)

To Walden to get its temperature. . . . So it appears that the bottom of Walden has, in fact, the temperature of a genuine and cold spring, or probably is of the same temperature with the average mean temperature of the earth. . . . Walden, then, must be included among the springs, but it is one which has no outlet,—is a well rather. It reaches down to where the temperature of the earth is unchanging. It is not a superficial pond,—not in the mere skin of the earth. It goes deeper.

AUGUST 28
JOURNAL (AUGUST 28, 1851)

The poet is a man who lives at last by watching his moods. An old poet comes at last to watch his moods as narrowly as a cat does a mouse.

AUGUST 29

JOURNAL (AUGUST 29, 1854)

Early for several mornings I have heard the sound of a flail. It leads me to ask if I have spent as industrious a spring and summer as the farmer, and gathered as rich a crop of experience. If so, the sound of my flail will be heard by those who have ears to hear, separating the kernel from the chaff all the fall and winter, and a sound no less cheering it will be. If the drought has destroyed the corn, let not all harvests fail.

AUGUST 30

JOURNAL (AUGUST 30, 1856)

I see that all is not garden and cultivated field and crops, that there are square rods in Middlesex County as purely primitive and wild as they were a thousand years ago, which have escaped the plow and the axe and the scythe and the cranberry-rake, little oases of wildness in the desert of our civilization, wild as a square rod on the moon. [THE ROD IS A SURVEYOR'S MEASURE, 16.5 FEET LONG.]

We commonly sacrifice to supper this serene and sacred hour. Our customs turn the hour of sunset to a trivial time, as at the meeting of two roads, one coming from the noon, the other leading to the night. It might be [well] if our repasts were taken out-of-doors, in view of the sunset and the rising stars; if there were two persons whose pulses beat together, if men cared for the Κόσμος [Cosmos], or *beauty* of the world; if men were *social* in a high and rare sense.

SEPTEMBER

It is time that we had uncommon schools, that we did not leave off our education when we begin to be men and women. It is time that villages were universities, and their elder inhabitants the fellows of universities, with leisure—if they are, indeed, so well off—to pursue liberal studies the rest of their lives. Shall the world be confined to one Paris or one Oxford forever? Cannot students be boarded here and get a liberal education under the skies of Concord?

"Reading," *Walden* (1854)

SEPTEMBER 1

JOURNAL (SEPTEMBER 2, 1856)

The botanist refers you, for . . . wild plants, further inland or westward to so many miles from Boston, as if Nature or the Indians had any such preferences. . . . As if there were primarily and essentially any more wildness in a western acre than an eastern one!

SEPTEMBER 2

JOURNAL (SEPTEMBER 2, 1851)

The body, the senses, must conspire with the mind. . . . Often I feel that my head stands out too dry, when it should be immersed. A writer, a man writing, is the scribe of all nature; he is the corn and the grass and the atmosphere writing. . . . Whatever things I perceive with my entire man, those let me record, and it will be poetry.

SEPTEMBER 3

"ECONOMY," WALDEN (1854)

I would not have any one adopt *my* mode of living on any account; for . . . I desire that there may be as many different persons in the world as possible; but I would have each one be very careful to find out

and pursue *his own* way, and not his father's or his mother's or his neighbor's instead.

SEPTEMBER 4
JOURNAL (SEPTEMBER 5, 1851)

All wisdom is the reward of a discipline, conscious or unconscious. . . . Cultivate reverence.

SEPTEMBER 5
JOURNAL (SEPTEMBER 5, 1851)

No doubt, like plants, we are fed through the atmosphere, and the varying atmospheres of various seasons of the year feed us variously. How often we are sensible of being thus fed and invigorated! And all nature contributes to this aerial diet its food of finest quality. . . . As Wilkinson says, ". . . This then, at least, is the office of the lungs—to drink the atmosphere with the planet dissolved in it."

SEPTEMBER 6
"CONCLUSION," *WALDEN* (1854)

I left the woods for as good a reason as I went there.

Perhaps it seemed to me that I had several more lives to live, and could not spare any more time for that one. [THOREAU LEFT WALDEN POND ON SEPTEMBER 6, 1847.]

SEPTEMBER 7
JOURNAL (SEPTEMBER 7, 1851)

I do not remember any page which will tell me how to spend this afternoon. I do not so much wish to know how to economize time as how to spend it, by what means to grow rich, that the day may not have been in vain. . . . My profession is to be always on the alert to find God in nature, to know his lurking-places, to attend all the oratorios, the operas, in nature.

SEPTEMBER 8
"SOLITUDE," *WALDEN* (1854)

When I return to my house I find that visitors have been there and left their cards, either a bunch of flowers, or a wreath of evergreen, or a name in pencil on a yellow walnut leaf or a chip. They who come rarely to the woods take some little piece of the forest into their hands to play with by the way, which they leave, either intentionally or accidentally. One has peeled a willow wand, woven it into a ring, and dropped it on my table.

SEPTEMBER 9

JOURNAL (SEPTEMBER 9, 1858)

It requires a different intention of the eye in the same locality to see different plants, as, for example, *Juncaceae* [rushes] and *Gramineae* [grasses] even; *i.e.*, I find that when I am looking for the former, I do not see the latter in their midst. How much more, then, it requires different intentions of the eye and of the mind to attend to different departments of knowledge! How differently the poet and the naturalist look at objects! A man sees only what concerns him.

SEPTEMBER 10

JOURNAL (SEPTEMBER 10, 1851)

Surely this earth is fit to be inhabited, and many enterprises may be undertaken with hope where so many young plants are pushing up. In the spring I burned over a hundred acres till the earth was sere and black, and by midsummer this space was clad in a fresher and more luxuriant green than the surrounding even. Shall man then despair? Is he not a sprout-land too, after never so many searings and witherings?

SEPTEMBER 11

America is said to be the arena on which the battle of freedom is to be fought; but surely it cannot be freedom in a merely political sense that is meant.... What is it to be free from King George and continue the slaves of King Prejudice? What is it to be born free and not to live free? What is the value of any political freedom, but as a means to moral freedom?

SEPTEMBER 12

I can hardly believe that there is so great a difference between one year and another as my journal shows. The 11th of this month last year, the river was as high as it commonly is in the spring, over the causeway on the Corner road. It is now quite low. Last year, October 9th, the huckleberries were fresh and abundant on Conantum. They are now already dried up.

SEPTEMBER 13

I must walk more with free senses. It is as bad to *study* stars and clouds as flowers and stones. I must

let my senses wander as my thoughts, my eyes see without looking. Carlyle said that how to observe was to look, but I say that it is rather to see, and the more you look the less you will observe. I have the habit of attention to such excess that my senses get no rest, but suffer from a constant strain. Be not preoccupied with looking. Go not to the object; let it come to you. . . . What I need is not to look at all, but a true sauntering of the eye.

SEPTEMBER 14

JOURNAL (SEPTEMBER 14, 1856)

How ever unexpected are these later flowers! You thought that Nature had about wound up her affairs. . . . You thought you knew every twig and leaf by the roadside, and nothing more was to be looked for there; and now, to your surprise, these ditches are crowded with millions of little stars. They suddenly spring up and face you, with their legions on each side the way, as if they had lain in ambuscade there. The flowering of the ditches. Call them travellers' thoughts, numerous though small, worth a penny at least. . . . A starry meteoric shower, a milky way, in the flowery kingdom in whose aisles we travel.

SEPTEMBER 15

A WEEK ON THE CONCORD AND
MERRIMACK RIVERS (1849)

As we lay awake long before daybreak, listening to the rippling of the river and the rustling of the leaves, in suspense whether the wind blew up or down the stream, was favorable or unfavorable to our voyage, we already suspected that there was a change in the weather, from a freshness as of autumn in these sounds. The wind in the woods sounded like an incessant waterfall dashing and roaring amid rocks, and we even felt encouraged by the unusual activity of the element. . . . That night was the turning-point in the season. We had gone to bed in summer, and we awoke in autumn; for summer passes into autumn in some unimaginable point of time, like the turning of a leaf. [RECALLING THE LAST NIGHT OF HENRY AND JOHN THOREAU'S RIVER VOYAGE, SEPTEMBER 15, 1839.]

SEPTEMBER 16

JOURNAL (SEPTEMBER 12, 1853)

It occurred to me when I awoke this morning, feeling regret for intemperance of the day before in eating fruit, which had dulled my sensibilities, that man was to be treated as a musical instrument, and if any viol was to be made of sound timber and kept well tuned always, it was he, so that when the bow

of events is drawn across him he may vibrate and resound in perfect harmony. A sensitive soul will be continually trying its strings to see if they are in tune.

SEPTEMBER 17
THE MAINE WOODS (1864)

As I sat before the fire on my fir-twig seat, without walls above or around me, I remembered how far on every hand that wilderness stretched . . . and wondered if any bear or moose was watching the light of my fire; for Nature looked sternly upon me on account of the murder of the moose. [ON SEPTEMBER 17, 1853, THOREAU PARTICIPATED IN HUNTING AND KILLING A MOOSE.]

SEPTEMBER 18
JOURNAL (SEPTEMBER 14, 1855)

It costs so much to publish, would it not be better for the author to put his manuscripts in a safe?

SEPTEMBER 19
JOURNAL (SEPTEMBER 19, 1858)

Hear a chewink's *chewink*. But how ineffectual is the note of a bird now! We hear it as if we heard it not,

and forget it immediately. In spring it makes its due impression, and for a long time will not have done echoing, as it were, through our minds. It is even as if the atmosphere were in an unfavorable condition for this kind of music. Every musician knows how much depends on this.

SEPTEMBER 20
JOURNAL (AUGUST 19, 1851)

The poet must be continually watching the moods of his mind, as the astronomer watches the aspects of the heavens. What might we not expect from a long life faithfully spent in this wise? The humblest observer would see some stars shoot. . . . It matters not whether they visit my mind or yours,—whether the meteor falls in my field or in yours,—only that it come from heaven.

SEPTEMBER 21
JOURNAL (SEPTEMBER 21, 1854)

I sometimes seem to myself to owe all my little success, all for which men commend me, to my vices. I am perhaps more willful than others and make enormous sacrifices, even of others' happiness, it may be, to gain my ends. It would seem even as if

nothing good could be accomplished without some vice to aid in it.

SEPTEMBER 22
JOURNAL (SEPTEMBER 22, 1852)

In love we impart, each to each, in subtlest immaterial form of thought or atmosphere, the best of ourselves, such as commonly vanishes or evaporates in aspirations, and mutually enrich each other. The lover alone perceives and dwells in a certain human fragrance. To him humanity is not only a flower, but an aroma and a flavor also.

SEPTEMBER 23
"THE BEAN-FIELD," *WALDEN* (1854)

I said to myself, I will not plant beans and corn with so much industry another summer, but such seeds, if the seed is not lost, as sincerity, truth, simplicity, faith, innocence, and the like, and see if they will not grow in this soil, even with less toil and manurance, and sustain me, for surely it has not been exhausted for these crops.

SEPTEMBER 24

JOURNAL (SEPTEMBER 24, 1859)

A man must attend to Nature closely for many years to know when, as well as where, to look for his objects, since he must always anticipate her a little. . . . I would know when in the year to expect certain thoughts and moods, as the sportsman knows when to look for plover.

SEPTEMBER 25

"AUTUMNAL TINTS" (1862)

Why, it takes a sharpshooter to bring down even such trivial game as snipes and woodcocks; he must take very particular aim, and know what he is aiming at. . . . And so is it with him that shoots at beauty; though he wait till the sky falls, he will not bag any, if he does not already know its seasons and haunts, and the color of its wing,—if he has not dreamed of it, so that he can *anticipate* it; then, indeed, he flushes it at every step.

SEPTEMBER 26

"SOLITUDE," *WALDEN* (1854)

Shall I not have intelligence with the earth? Am I not partly leaves and vegetable mould myself?

SEPTEMBER 27

JOURNAL (SEPTEMBER 27, 1852)

As I look northwestward to that summit from a Concord cornfield, how little can I realize all the life that is passing between me and it,—the retired up-country farmhouses, the lonely mills, wooded vales, wild rocky pastures, and new clearings on stark mountain-sides, and rivers gurgling through primitive woods! All these, and how much more, I *overlook*. I see the very peak,—there can be no mistake,—but how much I do not see, that is between me and it!

SEPTEMBER 28

"WALKING" (1862)

Every sunset which I witness inspires me with the desire to go to a West as distant and as fair as that into which the sun goes down. He appears to migrate westward daily, and tempt us to follow him.

SEPTEMBER 29

JOURNAL (SEPTEMBER 29, 1854)

One might say that all views through a telescope or microscope were purely visionary, for it is only by his eye and not by any other sense—not by his whole

man—that the beholder is there where he is presumed to be. It is a disruptive mode of viewing as far as the beholder is concerned.

SEPTEMBER 30

"SOUNDS," *WALDEN* (1854)

I am refreshed and expanded when the freight train rattles past me, and I smell the stores which go dispensing their odors all the way from Long Wharf to Lake Champlain, reminding me of foreign parts, of coral reefs, and Indian oceans, and tropical climes, and the extent of the globe.

OCTOBER

October answers to that period in the life of man when he is no longer dependent on his transient moods, when all his experience ripens into wisdom, but every root, branch, leaf of him glows with maturity. What he has been and done in his spring and summer appears. He bears his fruit.

Journal (November 14, 1853)

৩৩৩

OCTOBER 1

Now too, the first of October, or later, the elms are at the height of their autumnal beauty,—great brownish-yellow masses, warm from their September oven, hanging over the highway. Their leaves are perfectly ripe. I wonder if there is any answering ripeness in the lives of the men who live beneath them.

OCTOBER 2

"WALKING" (1862)

The landscape-painter uses the figures of men to mark a road. He would not make that use of my figure. I walk out into a nature such as the old prophets and poets, Menu, Moses, Homer, Chaucer, walked in. You may name it America, but it is not America; neither Americus Vespucius, nor Columbus, nor the rest were the discoverers of it.

OCTOBER 3

"SOLITUDE," *WALDEN* (1854)

Some of my pleasantest hours were during the long rain-storms in the spring or fall, which confined me to the house for the afternoon as well as the fore-

noon, soothed by their ceaseless roar and pelting; when an early twilight ushered in a long evening in which many thoughts had time to take root and unfold themselves.

OCTOBER 4

JOURNAL (OCTOBER 4, 1859)

It is only when we forget all our learning that we begin to know. I do not get nearer by a hair's breadth to any natural object so long as I presume that I have an introduction to it from some learned man. To conceive of it with a total apprehension I must for the thousandth time approach it as something totally strange. If you would make acquaintance with the ferns you must forget your botany. . . . You must be aware that *no thing* is what you have taken it to be.

OCTOBER 5

"WHERE I LIVED, AND WHAT I LIVED FOR," *WALDEN* (1854)

If we do not get out sleepers, and forge rails, and devote days and nights to the work, but go to tinkering upon our *lives* to improve *them*, who will build railroads? And if railroads are not built, how shall we get to heaven in season? But if we stay at home and

mind our business, who will want railroads? We do not ride on the railroad; it rides upon us.

OCTOBER 6

JOURNAL* (FALL–WINTER 1845–46)

To be a philosopher is not even to have subtle thoughts and found a school—but rarer still to live a life of simplicity—of independence—of magnanimity & trust—such as all men should live.

OCTOBER 7

JOURNAL (OCTOBER 7, 1842)

A little girl has just brought me a purple finch or American linnet. These birds are now moving south. It reminds me of the pine and spruce, and the juniper and cedar on whose berries it feeds. It has the crimson hues of the October evenings, and its plumage still shines as if it had caught and preserved some of their tints. . . . It reminds me of many things I had forgotten. Many a serene evening lies snugly packed under its wing.

OCTOBER 8

JOURNAL (OCTOBER 7, 1851)

The weeds being dead and the weather cooler, the water is more transparent. Now is the time to observe such weeds as have not been destroyed. The fishes are plainly seen. Saw a pickerel which had swallowed a smaller fish, with the tail projecting from his mouth. . . . There is a great difference between this season and a month ago,—warm as this happens to be,—as between one period of your life and another. A little frost is at the bottom of it.

OCTOBER 9

"WALKING" (1862)

I am alarmed when it happens that I have walked a mile into the woods bodily, without getting there in spirit. In my afternoon walk I would fain forget all my morning occupations and my obligations to society. But it sometimes happens that I cannot easily shake off the village. The thought of some work will run in my head and I am not where my body is,—I am out of my senses. In my walks I would fain return to my senses. What business have I in the woods, if I am thinking of something out of the woods?

But a government in which the majority rule in all cases cannot be based on justice, even as far as men understand it. Can there not be a government in which majorities do not virtually decide right and wrong, but conscience?—in which majorities decide only those questions to which the rule of expediency is applicable? Must the citizen ever for a moment, or in the least degree, resign his conscience to the legislator? Why has every man a conscience, then? I think that we should be men first, and subjects afterward.

OCTOBER 11

JOURNAL (OCTOBER 12, 1851)

I seem to be more constantly merged in nature; my intellectual life is more obedient to nature than formerly, but perchance less obedient to Spirit. I have less memorable seasons. I exact less of myself. I am getting used to my meanness, getting to accept my low estate. O if I could be discontented with myself! If I could feel anguish at each descent!

OCTOBER 12

The delicacy of the stratification in the white sand by the railroad [tracks], where they have been getting out sand for the brick-yards, the delicate stratification of this great globe like the leaves of the choicest volume just shut on a lady's table. The piled-up history! I am struck by the slow and delicate process by which the globe was formed.

OCTOBER 13

I hear Lincoln bell tolling for church. . . . Heard at a distance, the sound of a bell acquires a certain vibratory hum, as it were from the air through which it passes, like a harp. All music is a harp music at length, as if the atmosphere were full of strings vibrating to this music. It is not the mere sound of the bell, but the humming in the air, that enchants me . . . a sound which is very much modified, sifted, and refined before it reaches my ear.

OCTOBER 14

"HOUSE-WARMING," *WALDEN* (1854)

The wasps came by thousands to my lodge in October, as to winter quarters, and settled on my windows within and on the walls overhead, sometimes deterring visitors from entering. Each morning, when they were numbed with cold, I swept some of them out, but I did not trouble myself much to get rid of them; I even felt complimented by their regarding my house as a desirable shelter.

OCTOBER 15

JOURNAL (OCTOBER 15, 1859)

Each town should have a park, or rather a primitive forest, of five hundred or a thousand acres, where a stick should never be cut for fuel, a common possession forever, for instruction and recreation. . . . Let us keep the New World *new*, preserve all the advantages of living in the country.

OCTOBER 16

JOURNAL (OCTOBER 16, 1857)

A great part of the pine-needles have just fallen. See the carpet of pale-brown needles under this pine.

How light it lies up on the grass, and that great rock, and the wall, resting thick on its top and its shelves. . . . They are not yet flat and reddish, but a more delicate pale brown, and lie up light as joggle-sticks just dropped. The ground is nearly concealed by them. How beautifully they die, making cheerfully their annual contribution to the soil! They fall to rise again; as if they knew that it was not one annual deposit alone that made this rich mould in which pine trees grow.

OCTOBER 17

JOURNAL (OCTOBER 16, 1859)

Men attach a false importance to celestial phenomena as compared with terrestrial, as if it were more respectable and elevating to watch your neighbors than to mind your own affairs. The nodes of the stars are not the knots we have to untie.

OCTOBER 18

JOURNAL (OCTOBER 18, 1858)

This October festival costs no powder nor ringing of bells, but every tree is a liberty-pole on which a thousand bright flags are run up. . . . A village is not complete unless it has these trees to mark the season in it. They are as important as a town clock. Such a

village will not be found to work well. It has a screw loose; an essential part is wanting. Let us have willows for spring, elms for summer, maples and walnuts and tupelos for autumn, evergreens for winter, and oaks for all seasons. What is a gallery in a house to a gallery in the streets!

OCTOBER 19

JOURNAL (OCTOBER 19, 1859)

When a government puts forth its strength on the side of injustice, as ours (especially to-day) to maintain slavery and kill the liberators of the slave, what a merely brute, or worse than brute, force it is seen to be! A demoniacal force! It is more manifest than ever that tyranny rules. . . . High treason which is resistance to *tyranny* here below has its origin in, and is first committed by, the power that makes and forever re-creates man. [AFTER HEARING OF THE CAPTURE OF ABOLITIONIST JOHN BROWN.]

OCTOBER 20

JOURNAL* (FALL 1846)

All material things are in some sense man's kindred, and subject to the same laws with him.

Even a taper is his relative—and burns not eter-

nally, as some say of lamps found burning in ancient sepulchres—but only a certain number of his hours . . . completing its life within his own. . . . Not so those tapers the fixed stars which are not both lit and burnt out in the life of a man—yet they too are his distant relations.

OCTOBER 21
JOURNAL (OCTOBER 18, 1855)

How much beauty in decay! I pick up a white oak leaf, dry and stiff, but yet mingled red and green, October-like, whose pulpy part some insect has eaten beneath, exposing the delicate network of its veins. It is very beautiful held up to the light,—such work as only an insect eye could perform. Yet, perchance, to the vegetable kingdom such a revelation of ribs is as repulsive as the skeleton in the animal kingdom.

OCTOBER 22
JOURNAL (OCTOBER 22, 1858)

The oaks stand browned and crisped (amid the pines), their bright colors for the most part burnt out, like a loaf that is baked, and suggest an equal wholesomeness. The whole tree is now not only ripe but, as it were, a fruit perfectly cooked by the sun.

That same sun which called forth its leaves in the spring has now, aided by the frost, sealed up their fountains for the year and withered them. The order has gone forth for them to rest. As each tree casts its leaves it stands careless and free, like a horse freed from his harness . . . with concentrated strength and contentment, ready to brave the blasts of winter without a murmur.

OCTOBER 23

JOURNAL (OCTOBER 23, 1855)

Now is the time for chestnuts. A stone cast against the trees shakes them down in showers upon one's head and shoulders. But I cannot excuse myself for using the stone. . . . It is worse than boorish, it is criminal, to inflict an unnecessary injury on the tree that feeds or shadows us. Old trees are our parents, and our parents' parents, perchance. If you would learn the secrets of Nature, you must practice more humanity than others. The thought that I was robbing myself by injuring the tree did not occur to me, but I was affected as if I had cast a rock at a sentient being.

OCTOBER 24
"AUTUMNAL TINTS" (1862)

They that soared so loftily, how contentedly they return to dust again, and are laid low, resigned to lie and decay at the foot of the tree, and afford nourishment to new generations of their kind, as well as to flutter on high! They teach us how to die.

OCTOBER 25
JOURNAL (NOVEMBER 12, 1859)

There was a remarkable sunset, I think the 25th of October. The sunset sky reached quite from west to east, and it was the most varied in its forms and colors of any that I remember to have seen. At one time the clouds were most softly and delicately rippled, like the ripple-marks on sand. But it was hard for me to see its beauty then, when my mind was filled with Captain Brown. So great a wrong as his fate implied overshadowed all beauty in the world.

OCTOBER 26
JOURNAL (OCTOBER 27, 1857)

I go [sail] up the river as far as Hubbard's Second Grove, in order to share the general commotion and

excitement of the elements,—wind and waves and rain. . . . It was exciting to feel myself tossed by the dark waves and hear them surge about me. The reign of water now begins, and how it gambols and revels! Waves are its leaves, foam its blossoms. How they run and leap in great droves, deriving new excitement from each other! Schools of porpoises and blackfish are only more animated waves and have acquired the gait and game of the sea itself.

OCTOBER 27

JOURNAL (OCTOBER 27, 1855)

So there is one thought for the field, another for the house. I would have my thoughts, like wild apples, to be food for walkers, and will not warrant them to be palatable if tasted in the house.

OCTOBER 28

JOURNAL (OCTOBER 28, 1852)

The everlasting geometry of the stars. How incredible to be described are these bright points which appear in the blue sky as the darkness increases, said to be other worlds, like the berries on the hills when the summer is ripe!

OCTOBER 29

When the leaves fall, the whole earth is a cemetery pleasant to walk in. I love to wander and muse over them in their graves. Here are no lying nor vain epitaphs. What though you own no lot at Mount Auburn? Your lot is surely cast somewhere in this vast cemetery, which has been consecrated from of old. You need attend no auction to secure a place. There is room enough here. [ORIGINALLY WRITTEN ON OCTOBER 29, 1855.]

OCTOBER 30

JOURNAL (OCTOBER 26, 1853)

It is surprising how any reminiscence of a different season of the year affects us. When I meet with any such in my Journal, it affects me as poetry, and I appreciate that other season and that particular phenomenon more than at the time. The world so seen is all one spring, and full of beauty. . . . Only the rarest flavor, the purest melody, of the season thus comes down to us.

As I sit on the Cliff there, the sun is now getting low, and the woods in Lincoln south and east of me are lit up by its more level rays, and there is brought out a more brilliant redness in the scarlet oaks, scattered so equally over the forest, than you would have believed was in them. Every tree of this species which is visible in these directions, even to the horizon, now stands out distinctly red. . . . You see a redder tree than exists. It is a strong red, which gathers strength from the air on its way to your eye. It is partly borrowed fire, borrowed of the sun.

NOVEMBER

These apples have hung in the wind and frost and rain till they have absorbed the qualities of the weather or season, and thus are highly *seasoned*, and they *pierce* and *sting* and *permeate* us with their spirit. They must be eaten in *season*, accordingly,— that is, out-of-doors.

To appreciate the wild and sharp flavors of these October fruits, it is necessary that you be breathing the sharp October or November air. The outdoor air and exercise which the walker gets give a different tone to his palate, and he craves a fruit which the sedentary would call harsh and crabbed. They must be eaten in the fields, when your system is all aglow with exercise, when the frosty weather nips your fingers, the wind rattles the bare boughs or rustles the few remaining leaves, and the jay is heard screaming around. What is sour in the house a bracing walk makes sweet. Some of these apples might be labeled, "To be eaten in the wind."

"Wild Apples" (1862)

NOVEMBER 1

As the afternoons grow shorter, and the early evening drives us home to complete our chores, we are reminded of the shortness of life, and become more pensive, at least in this twilight of the year. . . . And yet there is no more tempting novelty than this new November. No going to Europe or another world is to be named with it. Give me the old familiar walk, post-office and all, with this ever new self, with this infinite expectation and faith, which does not know when it is beaten. We'll go nutting once more. We'll pluck the nut of the world, and crack it in the winter evenings.

NOVEMBER 2

What is Nature unless there is an eventful human life passing within her? Many joys and many sorrows are the lights and shadows in which she shows most beautiful.

NOVEMBER 3

THE MAINE WOODS (1864)

Perhaps our own woods and fields,—in the best wooded towns, where we need not quarrel about the huckleberries,—with the primitive swamps scattered here and there in their midst, but not prevailing over them, are the perfection of parks and groves, gardens, arbors, paths, vistas, and landscapes. They are the natural consequence of what art and refinement we as a people have,—the common which each village possesses, its true paradise, in comparison with which all elaborately and willfully wealth-constructed parks and gardens are paltry imitations.

[ORIGINALLY WRITTEN ON NOVEMBER 3, 1853.]

NOVEMBER 4

"AUTUMNAL TINTS" (1862)

There is just as much beauty visible to us in the landscape as we are prepared to appreciate,—not a grain more. The actual objects which one man will see from a particular hilltop are just as different from those which another will see as the beholders are different. The scarlet oak must, in a sense, be in your eye when you go forth. We cannot see anything until we are possessed with the idea of it, take it into our heads,—and then we can hardly see anything else.

[ORIGINALLY WRITTEN ON NOVEMBER 4, 1858.]

All voting is a sort of gaming, like checkers or back-gammon, with a slight moral tinge to it, a playing with right and wrong, with moral questions; and betting naturally accompanies it. The character of the voters is not staked. I cast my vote, perchance, as I think right; but I am not vitally concerned that that right should prevail. I am willing to leave it to the majority. . . . Even voting *for the right* is *doing* nothing for it. It is only expressing to men feebly your desire that it should prevail.

It is remarkable how little we attend to what is passing before us constantly, unless our genius directs our attention that way. There are these little sparrows with white in tail, perhaps the prevailing bird of late, which have flitted before me so many falls and springs, and yet they have been as it were strangers to me, and I have not inquired whence they came or whither they were going, or what their habits were.

NOVEMBER 7

JOURNAL (NOVEMBER 7, 1853)

This is the time for *our* best walnuts. . . . Got a peck and a half shelled. I did not wish to slight any of Nature's gifts. I am partial to the peculiar and wholesome sweetness of a nut, and I think that some time is profitably spent every autumn in gathering even such as our pignuts. Some of them are a very sizable, rich-looking, and palatable fruit. How can we expect to understand Nature unless we accept like children these her smallest gifts, valuing them more as her gifts than for their intrinsic value?

NOVEMBER 8

JOURNAL (NOVEMBER 8, 1858)

Each phase of nature, while not invisible, is yet not too distinct and obtrusive. It is there to be found when we look for it, but not demanding our attention. It is like a silent but sympathizing companion in whose company we retain most of the advantages of solitude, with whom we can walk and talk, or be silent, naturally, without the necessity of talking in a strain foreign to the place.

NOVEMBER 9

I, too, would fain set down something beside facts. Facts should only be as the frame to my pictures; they should be material to the mythology which I am writing; not facts to assist men to make money, farmers to farm profitably, in any common sense; facts to tell who I am, and where I have been or what I have thought: as now the bell rings for evening meeting, and its volumes of sound, like smoke which rises from where a cannon is fired, make the tent in which I dwell. . . . I would so state facts that they shall be significant, shall be myths or mythologic. Facts which the mind perceived, thoughts which the body thought,—with these I deal.

NOVEMBER 10

Politics is, as it were, the gizzard of society, full of grit and gravel, and the two political parties are its two opposite halves . . . which grind on each other. Not only individuals, but states, have thus a confirmed dyspepsia, which expresses itself, you can imagine by what sort of eloquence. [ORIGINALLY WRITTEN ON NOVEMBER 10, 1851.]

NOVEMBER 11

"CONCLUSION," *WALDEN* (1854)

Rather than love, than money, than fame, give me truth.

NOVEMBER 12

JOURNAL (NOVEMBER 12, 1853)

I cannot but regard it as a kindness in those who have the steering of me that, by the want of pecuniary wealth, I have been nailed down to this my native region so long and steadily, and made to study and love this spot of earth more and more. What would signify in comparison a thin and diffused love and knowledge of the whole earth instead, got by wandering? The traveller's is but a barren and comfortless condition. Wealth will not buy a man a home in nature.

NOVEMBER 13

JOURNAL (NOVEMBER 3, 1853)

I make it my business to extract from Nature whatever nutriment she can furnish me, though at the risk of endless iteration. I milk the sky and the earth.

NOVEMBER 14

My thought is a part of the meaning of the world, and hence I use a part of the world as a symbol to express my thought.

NOVEMBER 15

The seashore is a sort of neutral ground, a most advantageous point from which to contemplate this world. . . . The waves forever rolling to the land are too far-traveled and untamable to be familiar. Creeping along the endless beach amid the sun-squall and the foam, it occurs to us that we, too, are the product of sea-slime.

It is a wild, rank place, and there is no flattery in it.

NOVEMBER 16

I think that I cannot preserve my health and spirits, unless I spend four hours a day at least—and it is commonly more than that—sauntering through the woods and over the hills and fields, absolutely free from all worldly engagements. . . . I confess that I am astonished at the power of endurance, to say noth-

ing of the moral insensibility, of my neighbors who confine themselves to shops and offices the whole day for weeks and months, aye, and years almost together.

NOVEMBER 17

"WILD APPLES" (1862)

I fear that he who walks over these fields a century hence will not know the pleasure of knocking off wild apples. Ah, poor man, there are many pleasures which he will not know! . . . Now that they have grafted trees, and pay a price for them, they collect them into a plat by their houses, and fence them in,—and the end of it all will be that we shall be compelled to look for our apples in a barrel.

NOVEMBER 18

JOURNAL (NOVEMBER 17, 1858)

Ascending a little knoll covered with sweet-fern, shortly after, the sun appearing but a point above the sweet-fern, its light was reflected from a dense mass of the bare downy twigs of this plant in a surprising manner which would not be believed if described. It was quite like the sunlight reflected from grass and weeds covered with hoar frost. . . . A myriad of surfaces are now prepared to reflect the light. This

is one of the hundred silvery lights of November. The setting sun, too, is reflected from windows more brightly than at any other season. "November Lights" would be a theme for me.

NOVEMBER 19
JOURNAL (NOVEMBER 20, 1857)

The man who is often thinking that it is better to be somewhere else than where he is excommunicates himself. If a man is rich and strong anywhere, it must be on his native soil. Here I have been these forty years learning the language of these fields that I may the better express myself.

NOVEMBER 20
JOURNAL (NOVEMBER 20, 1858)

The glory of November is in its silvery, sparkling lights. . . . The air is so clear, and there are so many bare, polished, bleached or hoary surfaces to reflect the light. Few things are more exhilarating, if it is only moderately cold, than to walk over bare pastures and see the abundant sheeny light like a universal halo, reflected from the russet and bleached earth.

NOVEMBER 21

JOURNAL (NOVEMBER 22, 1853)

If there is any one with whom we have a quarrel, it is most likely that that one makes some just demand on us which we disappoint.

NOVEMBER 22

JOURNAL (NOVEMBER 22, 1860)

Though so many phenomena which we lately admired have now vanished, others are more remarkable and interesting than before. The smokes from distant chimneys, not only greater because more fire is required, but more distinct in the cooler atmosphere, are a very pleasing sight, and conduct our thoughts quickly to the roof and hearth and family beneath, revealing the homes of men.

NOVEMBER 23

JOURNAL (NOVEMBER 23, 1853)

What an engineer this water is! It comes with its unerring level, and reveals all the inequalities of the meadow. The farmer may see now what route to take to get the driest and firmest ground for his hay-carts,

how to cut his ditches, and where to drop more sand. It is an obvious piece of geometry in nature.

NOVEMBER 24

JOURNAL (NOVEMBER 24, 1860)

The bitter-sweet of a white oak acorn which you nibble in a bleak November walk over the tawny earth is more to me than a slice of imported pineapple. We do not think much of table-fruits. They are especially for aldermen and epicures. They do not feed the imagination. That would starve on them. These wild fruits, whether eaten or not, are a dessert for the imagination. The south may keep her pineapples, and we will be content with our strawberries.

NOVEMBER 25

JOURNAL (NOVEMBER 25, 1857)

This month taxes a walker's resources more than any. For my part, I should sooner think of going into quarters in November than in the winter. . . . It is but a short time, these afternoons, before the night cometh, in which no man can walk. If you delay to start till three o'clock, there will be hardly time left. . . . November Eat-heart,—is that the name of it? Not only the fingers cease to do their office, but

there is often a benumbing of the faculties generally. You can hardly screw up your courage to take a walk when all is thus tightly locked or frozen up and so little is to be seen in field or wood.

NOVEMBER 26

JOURNAL (NOVEMBER 24, 1857)

Some poets have said that writing poetry was for youths only, but not so. In that fervid and excitable season we only get the impulse which is to carry us onward in our future career. Ideals are then exhibited to us distinctly which all our lives after we may aim at but not attain. . . . In youth, when we are most elastic and there is a spring to us, we merely receive an impulse in the proper direction. To suppose that this is equivalent to having travelled the road, or obeyed the impulse faithfully throughout a lifetime, is absurd.

NOVEMBER 27

JOURNAL (NOVEMBER 27, 1857)

Standing before Stacy's large glass windows this morning, I saw that they were gloriously ground by the frost. I never saw such beautiful feather and fir-like frosting. His windows are filled with fancy arti-

cles and toys for Christmas and New-Year's presents, but this delicate and graceful outside frosting surpassed them all infinitely. I saw countless feathers with very distinct midribs and fine pinnae.... Other crystals looked like pine plumes the size of life. If glass could be ground to look like this, how glorious it would be!

NOVEMBER 28

JOURNAL (NOVEMBER 23, 1860)

Most of us are still related to our native fields as the navigator to undiscovered islands in the sea. We can any autumn discover a new fruit there which will surprise us by its beauty or sweetness.

NOVEMBER 29

"THE POND IN WINTER," *WALDEN* (1854)

Heaven is under our feet as well as over our heads.

NOVEMBER 30

JOURNAL (NOVEMBER 30, 1851)

A rather cold and windy afternoon, with some snow not yet melted on the ground. . . . Methinks that in

my mood I was asking Nature to give me a sign. I do not know exactly what it was that attracted my eye. I experienced a transient gladness, at any rate, at something which I saw. I am sure that my eye rested with pleasure on the white pines, now reflecting a silvery light, the infinite stories of their boughs, tier above tier, a sort of basaltic structure, a crumbling precipice of pine horizontally stratified. . . . Where is my home? It is indistinct as an old cellar-hole, now a faint indentation merely in a farmer's field . . . and I sit by the old site on the stump of an oak which once grew there. Such is the nature where we have lived.

[ON THE SITE OF HIS LONG-GONE WALDEN HOUSE.]

DECEMBER

Our village life would stagnate if it were not for the unexplored forests and meadows which surround it. We need the tonic of wildness,—to wade sometimes in marshes where the bittern and the meadow-hen lurk, and hear the booming of the snipe; to smell the whispering sedge where only some wilder and more solitary fowl builds her nest, and the mink crawls with its belly close to the ground. At the same time that we are earnest to explore and learn all things, we require that all things be mysterious and unexplorable, that land and sea be infinitely wild, unsurveyed and unfathomed by us because unfathomable. We can never have enough of nature. . . . We need to witness our own limits transgressed, and some life pasturing freely where we never wander.

"Spring," *Walden* (1854)

DECEMBER 1

Slate-colored snowbirds flit before me in the path, feeding on the seeds on the snow, the countless little brown seeds that begin to be scattered over the snow, so much the more obvious to bird and beast. A hundred kinds of indigenous grain are harvested now, broadcast upon the surface of the snow. Thus at a critical season these seeds are shaken down on to a clean white napkin, unmixed with dirt and rubbish, and off this the little pensioners pick them. Their clean table is thus spread a few inches or feet above the ground. Will wonder become extinct in me?

DECEMBER 2

"CIVIL DISOBEDIENCE" (1849)

But, to speak practically and as a citizen, unlike those who call themselves no-government men, I ask for, not at once no government, but *at once* a better government. Let every man make known what kind of government would command his respect, and that will be one step toward obtaining it.

DECEMBER 3

JOURNAL (DECEMBER 3, 1853)

The clam which I brought home the 30th [last month], and left outdoors by mistake, I now find frozen to death.... It is a somewhat saddening reflection that the beautiful colors of this shell for want of light cannot be said to exist, until its inhabitant has fallen a prey to the spoiler, and it is thus left a wreck upon the strand. Its beauty then beams forth, and it remains a splendid cenotaph to its departed tenant.

DECEMBER 4

JOURNAL* (AFTER DECEMBER 2, 1846)

Let the youth seize upon the finest and most memorable experience in his life—that which most reconciled him to his unknown destiny—and seek to discover in it his future path. Let him be sure that that way is his only true and worthy career.

DECEMBER 5

JOURNAL (DECEMBER 5, 1856)

I love the winter, with its imprisonment and its cold, for it compels the prisoner to try new fields and resources. . . . I love best to have each thing in its

season only, and enjoy doing without it at all other times. It is the greatest of all advantages to enjoy no advantage at all. I find it invariably true, the poorer I am, the richer I am. . . . While you are pleased to get knowledge and culture in many ways, I am delighted to think that I am getting rid of them. I have never got over my surprise that I should have been born into the most estimable place in all the world, and in the very nick of time, too.

DECEMBER 6

"HOUSE-WARMING," *WALDEN* (1854)

The next winter I used a small cooking-stove for economy, since I did not own the forest; but it did not keep fire so well as the open fireplace. Cooking was then, for the most part, no longer a poetic, but merely a chemic process. It will soon be forgotten, in these days of stoves, that we used to roast potatoes in the ashes, after the Indian fashion. The stove not only took up room and scented the house, but it concealed the fire, and I felt as if I had lost a companion.

DECEMBER 7

JOURNAL (DECEMBER 7, 1856)

That grand old poem called Winter is round again

without any connivance of mine. . . . The winters come now as fast as snowflakes. It is wonderful that old men do not lose their reckoning. It was summer, and now again it is winter. Nature loves this rhyme so well that she never tires of repeating it.

DECEMBER 8
JOURNAL (DECEMBER 8, 1854)

Winter has come unnoticed by me, I have been so busy writing. This is the life most lead in respect to Nature. How different from my habitual one! It is hasty, coarse, and trivial, as if you were a spindle in a factory. The other is leisurely, fine, and glorious, like a flower. In the first case you are merely getting your living; in the second you live as you go along.

DECEMBER 9
"THE SUCCESSION OF FOREST TREES" (1860)

Though I do not believe that a plant will spring up where no seed has been, I have great faith in a seed,—a, to me, equally mysterious origin for it. Convince me that you have a seed there, and I am prepared to expect wonders. I shall even believe that the millennium is at hand, and that the reign of justice is about to commence, when the Patent Office, or

Government, begins to distribute, and the people to plant, the seeds of these things.

DECEMBER 10
THE MAINE WOODS (1864)

The Anglo-American can indeed cut down, and grub up all this waving forest, and make a stump speech, and vote for Buchanan on its ruins, but he cannot converse with the spirit of the tree he fells, he cannot read the poetry and mythology which retire as he advances. He ignorantly erases mythological tablets in order to print his handbills and town-meeting warrants on them.

DECEMBER 11
"WINTER ANIMALS," *WALDEN* (1854)

Sometimes I heard the foxes as they ranged over the snow-crust, in moonlight nights, in search of a partridge or other game, barking raggedly and demoniacally like forest dogs, as if laboring with some anxiety, or seeking expression, struggling for light and to be dogs outright and run freely in the streets; for if we take the ages into our account, may there not be a civilization going on among brutes as well as men?

DECEMBER 12

JOURNAL (DECEMBER 12, 1856)

Wonderful, wonderful is our life and that of our companions! That there should be such a thing as a brute animal, not human! and that it should attain to a sort of society with our race! Think of cats, for instance. . . . They do not go to school, nor read the Testament; yet how near they come to doing so! how much they are like us who do so! What sort of philosophers are we, who know absolutely nothing of the origin and destiny of cats?

DECEMBER 13

JOURNAL (DECEMBER 13, 1857)

In sickness and barrenness it is encouraging to believe that our life is dammed and is coming to a head, so that there seems to be no loss, for what is lost in time is gained in power.

DECEMBER 14

THE MAINE WOODS (1864)

It is difficult to conceive of a region uninhabited by man. We habitually presume his presence and influence everywhere. And yet we have not seen pure

Nature, unless we have seen her thus vast and drear and inhuman, though in the midst of cities. . . . Here was no man's garden, but the unhandseled globe. It was not lawn, nor pasture, nor mead, nor woodland, nor lea, nor arable, nor waste land. It was the fresh and natural surface of the planet Earth, as it was made forever and ever,—to be the dwelling of man, we say,—so Nature made it, and man may use it if he can.

DECEMBER 15
JOURNAL (FEBRUARY 15, 1861)

A kitten is so flexible that she is almost double; the hind parts are equivalent to another kitten with which the fore part plays. She does not discover that her tail belongs to her till you tread upon it.

DECEMBER 16
JOURNAL (DECEMBER 16, 1837)

How indispensable to a correct study of Nature is a perception of her true meaning. The fact will one day flower out into a truth. The season will mature and fructify what the understanding had cultivated.

DECEMBER 17

The West of which I speak is but another name for the Wild; and what I have been preparing to say is, that in Wildness is the preservation of the world. Every tree sends its fibres forth in search of the Wild. The cities import it at any price. Men plow and sail for it. From the forest and wilderness come the tonics and barks which brace mankind. . . . I believe in the forest, and in the meadow, and in the night in which the corn grows.

DECEMBER 18

JOURNAL (DECEMBER 18, 1856)

At my lecture, the audience attended to me closely, and I was satisfied; that is all I ask or expect generally. Not one spoke to me afterward, nor needed they. I have no doubt that they liked it, in the main, though few of them would have dared say so, provided they were conscious of it. . . . Lectured in basement (vestry) of the orthodox church, and I trust helped to undermine it. [THE LECTURE HE DELIVERED WAS "WALKING."]

DECEMBER 19

JOURNAL (DECEMBER 19, 1856)

As I stand here, I hear the hooting of my old acquaintance the owl in Wheeler's Wood. . . . Heard here from out the depths of the wood, it sounds peculiarly hollow and drum-like, as if it struck on a tense skin drawn around, the tympanum of the wood, through which all we denizens of nature hear. Thus it comes to us an accredited and universal or melodious sound; is more than the voice of the owl, the voice of the wood as well. The owl only touches the stops, or rather wakes the reverberations. For all Nature is a musical instrument on which her creatures play.

DECEMBER 20

JOURNAL (DECEMBER 20, 1851)

Saw a large hawk circling over a pine wood below me, and screaming, apparently that he might discover his prey by their flight. Travelling ever by wider circles. What a symbol of the thoughts, now soaring, now descending, taking larger and larger circles, or smaller and smaller. It flies not directly whither it is bound, but advances by circles. . . . How it comes round, as with a wider sweep of thought! . . . Following its path, as it were through the vortices of the air. The poetry of motion. Not as preferring one place to another, but enjoying each as long as possible.

DECEMBER 21

Critical acumen is exerted in vain to uncover the past; the *past* cannot be *presented*; we cannot know what we are not. But one veil hangs over past, present, and future, and it is the province of the historian to find out, not what was, but what is.

DECEMBER 22

I have seen, in the form, in the expression of face, of a child three years old, the tried magnanimity and grave nobility of ancient and departed worthies. Just saw a little Irish boy, come from the distant shanty in the woods over the bleak railroad to school this morning, take his last step from his last snow-drift on to the schoolhouse door-step, floundering still. . . . Little Johnny Riordan, who faces cold and routs it like a Persian army, who, yet innocent, carries in his knees the strength of a thousand Indras. . . . While the charitable waddle about cased in furs, he, lively as a cricket, passes them on his way to school.

DECEMBER 23

A WEEK ON THE CONCORD AND MERRIMACK RIVERS (1849)

It is easier to discover another such a new world as Columbus did, than to go within one fold of this which we appear to know so well; the land is lost sight of, the compass varies, and mankind mutiny; and still history accumulates like rubbish before the portals of nature. But there is only necessary a moment's sanity and sound senses, to teach us that there is a nature behind the ordinary, in which we have only some vague preëmption right and western reserve as yet. We live on the outskirts of that region.

DECEMBER 24

JOURNAL (DECEMBER 24, 1841)

I want to go soon and live away by the pond, where I shall hear only the wind whispering among the reeds. It will be success if I shall have left myself behind. But my friends ask what I will do when I get there. Will it not be employment enough to watch the progress of the seasons?

DECEMBER 25

I learned this, at least, by my experiment; that if one advances confidently in the direction of his dreams, and endeavors to live the life which he has imagined, he will meet with a success unexpected in common hours. . . . If you have built castles in the air, your work need not be lost; that is where they should be. Now put the foundations under them.

DECEMBER 26

A man receives only what he is ready to receive, whether physically or intellectually or morally, as animals conceive at certain seasons their kind only. We hear and apprehend only what we already half know. . . . Every man thus *tracks himself* through life, in all his hearing and reading and observation and travelling. His observations make a chain. The phenomenon or fact that cannot in any wise be linked with the rest which he has observed, he does not observe. By and by we may be ready to receive what we cannot receive now.

DECEMBER 27

JOURNAL (DECEMBER 27, 1858)

The man of genius knows what he is aiming at; nobody else knows. And he alone knows when something comes between him and his object. In the course of generations, however, men will excuse you for not doing as they do, if you will bring enough to pass in your own way.

DECEMBER 28

JOURNAL (DECEMBER 28, 1852)

A broad margin of leisure is as beautiful in a man's life as in a book. . . . Keep the time, observe the hours of the universe, not of the cars. . . . How much, what infinite, leisure it requires, as of a lifetime, to appreciate a single phenomenon! You must camp down beside it as for life, having reached your land of promise, and give yourself wholly to it.

DECEMBER 29

JOURNAL (DECEMBER 29, 1851)

How admirable it is that we can never foresee the weather,—that that is always novel! Yesterday nobody dreamed of to-day; nobody dreams of to-

morrow. Hence the weather is ever the news. What a fine and measureless joy the gods grant us thus, letting us know nothing about the day that is to dawn!

DECEMBER 30

All day a driving snow-storm, imprisoning most, stopping the cars, blocking up the roads. No school to-day. . . . I wade to the post-office as solitary a traveller as ordinarily in a wood-path in winter. The snow is mid-leg deep, while drifts as high as one's head are heaped against the houses and fences, and here and there range across the street like snowy mountains. . . . It is as if the inhabitants were all frozen to death, and now you threaded the desolate streets weeks after that calamity. . . . Yet they are warmer, merrier than ever there within. At the post-office they ask each traveller news of the cars,—"Is there any train up or down?"—or how deep the snow is on a level.

DECEMBER 31

"WALKING" (1862)

So we saunter toward the Holy Land; till one day the sun shall shine more brightly than ever he has done, shall perchance shine into our minds and hearts,

and light up our whole lives with a great awakening light, as warm and serene and golden as on a bank-side in Autumn.

Index of Sources

July 6, July 7, July 11, July 18, August 7, August 10, August 24, August 25, September 13, September 22, September 27, October 12, October 28, November 14, December 28

Vol. 5: March 5–November 30, 1853, March 12, March 18, March 19, March 20, March 21, April 5, April 7, May 10, May 11, May 15, June 19, June 22, July 26, July 27, August 9, August 14, August 16, August 19, August 23, September 16, October (general), October 30, November 2, November 6, November 7, November 12, November 13, November 21, November 23

Vol. 6: December 1, 1853–August 31, 1854, January 1, January 11, January 16, January 26, January 30, January 31, February 17, March 5, April 2, April 12, April 25, May 6, May 9, May 17, May 22, May 28, May 29, June 15, June 16, June 17, July 3, July 28, August 3, August 5, August 22, August 29, December 3, December 30

Vol. 7: September 1, 1854–October 30, 1855, January 12, February 3, February 4, February 7, February 18, February 21, March 8, June 10, September 18, September 21, September 29, October 21, October 23, October 27, December 8

Vol. 8: November 1, 1855–August 15, 1856, January 6, January 18, March 23, April 6, April 28

Vol. 9: August 16, 1856–August 7, 1857, February 20, May 1, June 5, June 6, August 30, September 1, September 14, December 1, December 5, December 7, December 12, December 18, December 19

Vol. 10: August 8, 1857–June 29, 1858, January 5, January 24, March 17, March 30, October 16, October 26, November 19, November 25, November 26, November 27, December 13

Vol. 11: July 2, 1858–February 28, 1859, August 6, September 9, September 19, October 18, October 22, October 31, November 1, November 8, November 18, November 20, December 27

Vol. 12: March 2, 1859–November 30, 1859, March 2, March 13, March 24, March 27, March 28, September 24, October 4,

Note on the Text

Excerpts from Thoreau's writings are quoted from the 1906 publication of Thoreau's collected works by Houghton Mifflin, checked against the modern standard edition of Thoreau's works being published by Princeton University Press. The 1906 edition is widely reprinted and available online; the Princeton edition includes *Cape Cod* (1988) and *The Maine Woods* (1972), both edited by Joseph J. Moldenhauer; *Walden* (1971), edited by J. Lyndon Shanley; and *A Week on the Concord and Merrimack Rivers* (1980), edited by Carl F. Hovde, William L. Howarth, and Elizabeth Hall Witherell, with an introduction by Linck C. Johnson. Thoreau's essays "Civil Disobedience" (a.k.a. "Resistance to Civil Government") and "Life without Principle" may be found in *Cape Cod and Miscellanies* (1906) and in *Reform Papers* (1973), edited by Wendell Glick, which also includes "Reform and the Reformers." Thoreau's nature essays "Autumnal Tints," "Natural History of Massachusetts," "The Succession of Forest Trees," "Walking," "A Walk to Wachusett," "Wild Apples," "A Winter Walk," and "A Yankee in Canada" are all collected in *Excursions and Poems* (1906) and in *Excursions* (2007), edited by Joseph J. Moldenhauer. Most excerpts from Thoreau's journal are quoted from the 1906 Houghton

Mifflin series edited by Bradford Torrey and Francis Allen (14 vols.); excerpts marked by an asterisk are quoted by permission from the Princeton series editions, *Journal, Volume 2: 1842–1848* (1984), *Journal, Volume 3: 1848–1851* (1990), and *Journal, Volume 6: 1853* (2000), all edited by Robert Sattelmeyer.

The extract in the foreword from *Wild Fruits* is quoted from *Wild Fruits: Thoreau's Rediscovered Last Manuscript* (New York: Norton, 2000), recovered and edited by the great Thoreauvian Bradley P. Dean.